THE ART OF THE CATAPULT

Build GREEK BALLISTAE, ROMAN ONAGERS, ENGLISH TREBUCHETS, AND MORE ANCIENT ARTILLERY

WILLIAM GURSTELLE

CHICAGO
REVIEW
PRESS

Published by Chicago Review Press, Incorporated
814 North Franklin Street
Chicago, Illinois 60610
ISBN 978-0-912777-33-7

For more information, visit www.ArtOf TheCatapult.com

Library of Congress Cataloging-in-Publication Data

Names: Gurstelle, William, author.
Title: The art of the catapult : build Greek ballistae, Roman onagers,
  English trebuchets, and more ancient artillery / William Gurstelle.
Description: Second edition. | Chicago, Illinois : Chicago Review Press,
  [2018] | Includes bibliographical references and index.
Identifiers: LCCN 2018013851 (print) | LCCN 2018017438 (ebook) | ISBN
  9780912777344 (adobe pdf) | ISBN 9780912777351 (epub) | ISBN 9780912777368
  (kindle) | ISBN 9780912777337 (trade paper)
Subjects: LCSH: Catapult--History--Juvenile literature. | Catapult--Design
  and construction--Juvenile literature. | Ballista--History--Juvenile
  literature. | Ballista--Design and construction--Juvenile literature. |
  Weapons, Ancient--Juvenile literature. | Weapons, Ancient--Design and
  construction--Juvenile literature.
Classification: LCC U875 (ebook) | LCC U875 .G87 2018 (print) | DDC
  623.4/41--dc23
LC record available at https://lccn.loc.gov/2018013851

Cover design: Andrew J. Brozyna
Interior design: Jonathan Hahn
Interior layout: Andrew J. Brozyna
Interior illustrations: Laura D'Argo and Casimir Sienkiewicz; Damien Scogin

Printed in the United States of America
5 4 3 2 1

This book is dedicated to the authors of the books I enjoyed so much when I was younger, and still do today.

In particular, H. H. Windsor (*The Boy Mechanic*), William Allan Brooks (*Fun for Boys*), Don Herbert (*Mr. Wizard's Experiments for Young Scientists*), Joseph H. Adams (*Harper's Electricity Book for Boys*), and Daniel Carter Beard (*The American Boy's Handy Book*).

Except for Don Herbert, these men wrote their books in the 1940s and before. Happily, times have changed, and if these great authors were still at work, girls would certainly be included in the audience for such terrific activities as well as in their book titles.

CONTENTS

TIMELINE

399 *BCE*   The earliest catapults, which were large tension (bow-powered) catapults first used by Syracusean Greeks

340 *BCE*   Craftsmen working for Philip of Macedon build the first torsion-powered (coiled rope spring) ballistae

332 *BCE*   Alexander the Great besieges the island fortress of Tyre using rock-throwing torsion-powered ballistae

146 *BCE*   Roman historian Livy writes that over 400 onagers and ballistae were used at the Roman siege of Carthage

63 *BCE*   Roman legions make frequent use of onager or Wild Donkey style catapults in the battle for Jerusalem

67 *CE*   Roman General Vespasian uses onager catapults to besiege Jotapata

380   First written mention of catapult slings on Roman torsion-powered onagers.

500-600   First use of gravity-powered catapults, or trebuchets, by Chinese armies

600-900   Trebuchet technology slowly moves westward from the Far East to countries of the Near East and then to Europe

800	Traction, or human-powered, catapults come into widespread usage in European sieges
885	Vikings besiege the city of Paris using catapults
1191	More than 300 human-powered (traction) and rope-spring-powered (torsion) catapults used by Richard the Lionheart at the Siege of Acre during the Third Crusade
1200	Beginning of widespread trebuchet usage in European sieges
1204	Philip Augustus of France takes Chateau Gaillard from John of England using Cabulus, the Great Horse Catapult (trebuchet)
1268	Isma'il of Hilla and Ala al-Din of Mosul build the hui-hui pao catapult for Kublai Khan
1304	Edward I of England builds the enormous trebuchet he calls Ludgar, the War Wolf, to defeat the Scots at Stirling Castle
1305-1330	Period of John Crabbe's career as pirate and catapult builder in Flanders, Scotland, and England
1333	Don Alonso Teorio attempts to break the siege of Gibraltar by hurling sacks of flour to starving fortress defenders
1380-1480	Cannon and other gunpowder-based artillery supplant catapults in Europe
1480	Last recorded successful use of catapults in warfare at the Siege of Rhodes by Greeks against the attacking Turkish forces
1521	Last recorded unsuccessful use of a trebuchet in warfare, built by soldiers of Hernando Cortez during the Conquest of Mexico

Introduction

THE DAYS BEFORE GUNPOWDER

The rocks of the hills, taken and shaped by hard work,
Are made to soar forward from the sling of a machine;
Through wind and clouds they ride upon their way,
Like meteors, they thunder through space
                    —Unknown Chinese poet, 1300

In the days before gunpowder was invented, ancient military commanders used large, powerful throwing machines to help them lay siege to castles and forts. Warring countries would often invade each other with the aim of taking land, riches, and treasure from their neighbors. To prevent attackers from invading them and causing trouble, rulers raised armies, trained warriors, and, most important, built forts and castles for protection. Some of these forts had stone walls several feet thick and were surrounded by deep moats with drawbridges. The forts were built on high ground, allowing the defenders to look down upon attacking armies and fend them off by throwing spears, shooting arrows, and hurling stones at them. Attacking a castle was a hard job, and not one to be taken lightly. The invaders would need a lot of motivation, courage, and luck to have any chance at success.

Despite the protection provided by a fort or castle, wars and invasions were frequent. Political troubles, greed, and the power struggles of kings and princes often turned into armed military confrontations between kingdoms, regions, and cities. And, when men's thoughts turned to making war, they also turned to thoughts of building machines for winning the war. How did ancient warriors attack a fortified castle and win, before the days of cannons, airplanes, and tanks?

If you went back in time to, say, 400 BCE (that's about 2,400 years ago), you'd find that although the armies were smaller and the weapons used were more primitive, war was still war. Neighbors still fought with their neighbors. As far back as 400 bce, military leaders instructed their engineers to build large and powerful machines, called siege engines, that were capable of flinging gigantic projectiles and overcoming the protection afforded by castles and forts. From simple beginnings, these machines soon developed into marvelous, powerful, and complicated mechanisms. Given enough time and enough people to work them, they had the power to batter down the doors or walls of a fortress. But instead of using gunpowder or explosives like modern cannons do, they used enormous bows, big wooden or twisted rope springs, or heavy weights to toss the ammunition.

This book is about these machines, called catapults—the ancient artillery of the Greek, Roman, Chinese, Arab, and European armies. Besides learning about the machines, you will also hear about the lives and times of the best known and most famous of the warriors and kings who used catapults: Alexander the Great, ruler of Macedonia and the greatest of all the ancient Greek kings; Saladin, the mighty sultan of Egypt; John Crabbe of Flanders, pirate, adventurer, and consummate catapult builder; and Philip Augustus, King of France and antagonist of the English kings Richard (the Lionheart) and John. All these men, as well as the others described, were intimately involved in the design of catapults and were supremely talented in using them in battle.

Through their eyes you will be able to acquire an appreciation for how important, powerful, and interesting these devices are.

In the following sections of this book, there are plans for constructing your own scale models of these ancient marvels, as well as many related projects.

These machines had a lot of different names. The Greeks called them ballistae (plural of ballista), and the Romans called theirs onagers. The English and French armies of the Middle Ages called them trebuchets. The Chinese looked at their mechanical artillery and labeled them hsuan feng (whirlwind). The Turks dubbed their machines "witches with ropes for hair." In other parts of the world and at other times they were called mangonels, petraries, scorpions, and tormenta (plural for tormentum). But whatever the name given them by their builders, they were basically all catapults, built by military engineers to make something big go whoosh, and then splat.

Catapults were complicated, intricately crafted, powerful engines, capable of breaking up the walls of fortresses by launching heavy rocks through the air. The ancient catapult crews could hurl shot after shot against castle walls and doors. They could toss barrels of sticky, flaming goo over a city's protective walls and into the streets and courtyards of the city within them. They could fire large and heavy spears and arrows, far larger than could be launched by a simple bow and arrow, and by doing so they could change the course of a battle with only a few shots.

1

ALWAYS BE CAREFUL

The catapults and related projects described in this book have been designed with your safety foremost in mind. However, as you try them out, there is still a possibility that something unexpected may occur. It is important that you understand neither the author, the publisher, nor the bookseller can or will guarantee your safety. When you try the projects described here, you do so at your own risk.

Most of the projects and plans contained here are safe for children in late grade school on up to adult ages. But a few of the projects result in powerful siege engines with projectiles that can move pretty fast. So you should be aware that each city, town, or municipality has its own rules and regulations, some of which may apply to a few of the projects described in this book. Further, local authorities have wide latitude to interpret the law. Therefore, you should take time to understand the rules, regulations, and laws of the area in which you plan to carry out these projects. A check with local law enforcement can tell whether the project is suitable for your area. If not, there are plenty of other places where all of the items here can be undertaken safely and legally. If in doubt, be sure to check it out!

GENERAL SAFETY RULES
AND SUGGESTIONS

These are your general safety rules. Each project may also have its own specific safety instructions.

1. The building projects described here run the gamut from simple to complex. The purpose of most of the projects in this book is to build a device that throws something. So, the projects contained here should always be supervised by adults.

2. Read the entire project description carefully before beginning the construction process. Make sure you understand what the project is about, and what it is that you are trying to accomplish. If something is unclear, reread the directions until you fully comprehend it.

3. Some of the projects call for the use of hand tools or power tools. All tools must be used according to manufacturer recommendations. Saws and chisels are sharp, so handle them with caution and under adult supervision.

4. The area in which the catapult and related projects are operated must be cleared of ALL items that can be damaged by projectiles, flying objects, and so forth.

5. Keep people away from the firing zone near catapults, trebuchets, ballistae, slings, and flingers. Use care when transporting, aiming, and firing, and always be aware of where the device is pointing.

6. Wear protective eyewear when appropriate.

PLEASE, REMEMBER THIS:

1. The instructions and information are provided here for your use without any guarantee of safety. Each project has been extensively tested in a variety of conditions. But variations, mistakes, and unforeseen circumstances can and do occur; therefore, all projects and experiments are performed at your own risk. If you don't agree with this, then put this book down and find another activity that is more suitable.

2. And finally: there is no substitute for your own common sense. If something doesn't seem right, stop and review what's going on. You must take responsibility for your personal safety and the safety of others around you.

All of the projects in this book require adult supervision and each has its own unique safety requirements as well. Watch for these icons so you know what to expect:

 Use protective eyewear

Swinging arm alert: Watch out for moving arms or levers

Sharp and/or heavy tool advisory: Project requires use of saw or hammer

Flying object alert: Use care when aiming and firing

2

THE SCIENCE
OF SIEGE

From the earliest days of organized warfare, armies have always had three basic types of fighting units. These include first, infantry units that consist of men on foot who attempt to advance and take land and position against enemy forces. Second, cavalry units consisting of faster moving, highly mobile combat groups support the infantry. In past times, the cavalry used horses to make them speedy and mobile. Today, the cavalry have given up horses for tanks. And some armies today use something called "air cavalry," or the equivalent of flying tanks—heavily armored helicopters. And last, there are artillery units, groups of highly trained soldiers that set up and fire big guns to destroy fixed military targets such as buildings and encampments.

Modern artillery units are made up of howitzers, cannons, and rocket-firing batteries. The artillery soldiers are different from the infantry and the cavalry. First of all, they are not particularly fast moving or mobile. They go to a particular location, set up their guns, and then fire away. Second of all, they are especially effective against fixed targets—buildings, bridges, gun emplacements, and so forth.

Before the days of gunpowder and iron or steel cannon barrels, siege engines (catapults) were the artillery of the ancient armies. They were the primitive yet elegant equivalents of the cannons and howitzers used in modern armies. And, like cannons, siege engines weren't very mobile compared with the infantry soldiers or cavalry. In fact, the larger catapults, such as big trebuchets, would take weeks, sometimes even months to assemble in place. They had a narrowly defined but very important job to do. They were used to break down the walls of castles in a siege.

WARFARE IN ANCIENT TIMES

There were two broad kinds of military action during the age of catapults—the pitched battle and the siege. A pitched battle was just what it sounds like—soldiers on a battlefield, running, using their weapons, accomplishing specific objectives, hopefully under the direction of their commanding officers. If they were successful, they would gain territory and advantage and, in the process, defeat the opposing army. Certainly, ancient warfare was tough and brutal. Hand-to-hand combat, frontal assaults, skirmishing—these were the simple tactics employed in pitched battles from the Battle of Marathon in 490 BCE continuing through the time of the Roman Empire, and on into the Middle Ages. Many of these tactics of ancient warfare are still used in warfare today.

During classical times (the time of the ancient Greeks and Romans) and medieval times, as now, the soldiers used a variety of weapons in a pitched battle. In those days armies used spears, pikes, swords, daggers, slings and stones, battle-axes, clubs, and bows and arrows.

The other basic type of military action, besides a pitched battle, was the siege. When one side had a big advantage over the other side in terms of manpower or equipment, the other side could wisely choose to not meet the enemy on the field of battle, but instead retreat to the safety of a walled city, fortress, or castle. Here, within thick protective fortress walls made of limestone, sandstone, or flint, the defenders could hole up for months and, depending on the supply of food and water within, perhaps outlast the enemy encamped beyond the walls.

A castle was more than just a place of refuge. It was also the residence of a nobleman, a home base for an army, a headquarters of the area's commerce and industry, and the highest, strongest place around to beat off an attacker. Castles had walls several feet thick made of solid stone, with several different layers of architectural protection, such as walls, towers, and moats.

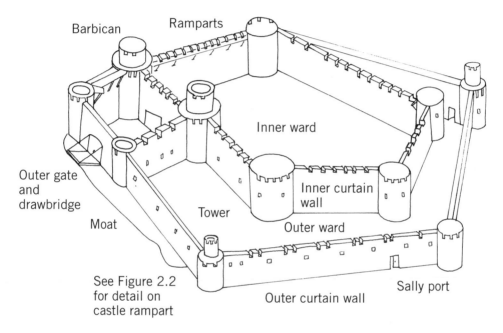

2.1 A typical castle layout.

It was hard to capture a castle, but if that's what the military leaders needed to do, armies would try to do it. The attackers could either try to wait out the defenders and force them to surrender by starving them, or they could lay siege to the castle.

If you visit a castle today, such as Stirling Castle in Scotland, Chateau Gaillard in France, or Bodrum Castle in Turkey, the graceful walls sitting atop a towering hill might give you an impression that a castle was designed for a simple strategy of passive defense, a place of safety where the defenders would hunker down behind the walls and simply try to outlast the attacking army. But this was not the case.

Certainly, the castle was designed and sited to make it as difficult to conquer for unfriendly armies as possible. But beyond that, castles were designed with entry and exit doors called sally ports so that the defenders within could come and go, unseen and secretly, to engage the enemy and then quickly retreat back into the safety of the castle. And perhaps most important, since the castle controlled the high ground, the archers and spearmen within the castle could confidently prevent the movement of enemy troops on the roads and pathways that it overlooked.

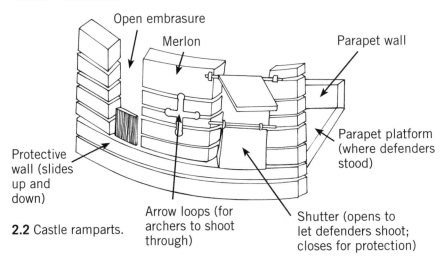

2.2 Castle ramparts.

Up on the ramparts—the platforms built high up on the castle walls—the defenders could look out at the attackers and shoot arrows and stones through openings called embrasures and arrow loops. For protection from the attackers, arrows, and missiles, they could hide behind thick stone coverings, called merlons, or heavy wooden or metal shutters.

For all these reasons, it was just not militarily feasible for an invading army to simply bypass a castle and continue on. An unconquered castle could not be ignored—it would have to be dealt with before the invading troops could go any further.

So, what were the tools and tactics that generals used to lay siege and conquer a castle? There were several well-known techniques, none of them guaranteed to be successful or easy to use. One method was called a blockade, which involved simply surrounding the castle with troops and ships and preventing any food or supplies from getting in.

A blockade sometimes worked, but often the garrison (the group of soldiers within a fortress or castle) was better supplied than the attacking army and could outlast the besiegers.

Another way was to use threats and bribery. The concepts of loyalty and national identity were somewhat different in ancient and medieval times than they are now. A commander could sometimes be persuaded to change sides, or maybe at least to give up, if the attackers made their threats fearful enough. The threats were usually crude and brutal—but the message was always simple and clear: surrender or else! For instance, at the siege of a castle in Crema, Italy, the attacking army, commanded by the German Emperor Frederick Barbarossa, took captured soldiers, cut off their heads, and then played games with them, tossing the heads like footballs from hand to hand in view of the besieged in the castle. The defenders within the castle went mad with rage when they saw this; they took the prisoners they had in their control and ripped them limb from limb on the castle ramparts. What a terrible time to be a soldier!

2.3 Heads were often used as projectiles.

Conversely, the castellan (the leader of the castle and the king's loyal man) might capitulate if certain promises of safety, payment, and bounty were provided. If the castellan truly was loyal and couldn't be bribed, then the besiegers might also consider gaining the castle

2.4 Storming the castle from a movable tower.

through the use of spies or inciting a mutiny among the rest of the defenders.

If starvation, negotiation, treachery, or threats were unsuccessful, then the only way left was to make an all-out attack on the castle. Daily catapult bombardment could reduce even a thick wall to rubble.

Day after day, night after night, the great swinging arms of the siege engines outside the walls would pound the stone guardians of the castle. And often, from inside the walls, great stone balls would answer back from the defender's own catapults, aimed directly at the attackers' stone throwers. Eventually the walls would start to break apart under the onslaught of heavy rock missiles: first a crack, then a fracture, then a hole. Once openings appeared that were large enough to move a soldier through, the main frontal assault could begin.

On a commander's order, the troops would rush toward the castle, shouting a war cry. An attack on a castle or fortress involved a short but furious battle, with soldiers attacking holes in the walls with picks and hammers and rushing through as soon as the openings were large enough. Simultaneously others would charge the wall with scaling ladders and attempt to climb up and over the castle walls to engage the defenders in direct and bloody combat. These were desperate fights indeed.

Another well-known method was to build a movable tower that was high enough to get men over the castle walls. These contraptions, built from wood and covered with animal hides, were built just slightly higher than the castle walls. They were called siege towers, and some were so big—four or five stories tall—that acres of woodlands were chopped down to make the boards to build them. When the time was right, the commanding knights would order the siege tower rolled into place, as close to the castle as possible. Then a front-facing door would open and a bridge would be lowered to enable the fighting men to rush forward into the castle.

Sometimes the attacking army would send in miners. These were men who worked underground, spending weeks or months digging with shovels in dark and airless tunnels underneath the walls of the castle. As they dug, they would prop up the tunnel walls with timbers to prevent them from collapsing. During the time of the actual attack, soldiers could then go underneath the walls and surprise the besieged by popping up in the middle of the castle grounds.

Or the miners would dig away the earth directly under the heavy castle wall. When enough dirt was removed, the wall would collapse into the hole and allow the besiegers to rush into the breach (a hole in a castle wall). Mining was one of the most effective ways to get inside a well-protected castle. Throughout history there is ample evidence that no castle could hold out for long once the miners got their picks in.

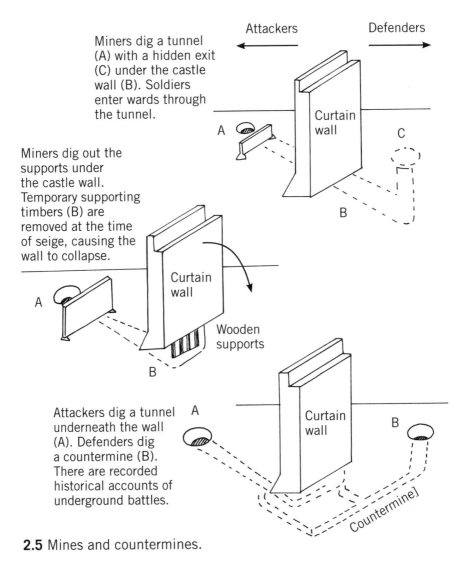

Miners dig a tunnel (A) with a hidden exit (C) under the castle wall (B). Soldiers enter wards through the tunnel.

Miners dig out the supports under the castle wall. Temporary supporting timbers (B) are removed at the time of seige, causing the wall to collapse.

Attackers dig a tunnel underneath the wall (A). Defenders dig a countermine (B). There are recorded historical accounts of underground battles.

2.5 Mines and countermines.

There were other more basic forms of assault as well. If brave, numerous, and motivated enough, the attackers could simply storm the fortress or castle gates or swim the moat. But most of all, the attackers would rush in through breaches in the thick castle walls caused by missiles—the large rocks hurled by the catapults.

Castle storming was difficult, exhausting, and horrifying. The men at arms must storm the castle, running and dodging missiles, holding bucklers (shields) overhead, all the while trying to climb a narrow scaling ladder. It took courage and fortitude to be a medieval fighting man. At the time of the siege, urged on by their leaders, the fighters would move to the perimeter of the fortress.

2.6 Storming the castle.

There, at the base of the walls, the attackers would shout out their war cry—"St. George! For England!" yelled the English; "For St. Andrew!" rejoined the Scots. "A Mat!" shouted the Spanish; and "Tue, Tue, Montjoye St. Denis!" cried out the French. The air would fill with the clamor of men, machines, and horses. The shouted exhortations and commands from the officers would mix with the agonized screams of the injured and the war cries of the foot soldiers, until they all combined into one great cacophonous roar of voices and clashing metal and the sound of falling walls, weapons, and men.

Certainly the siege was the most deadly, intense form of classical and medieval warfare. Under the cover of shields held overhead, the attackers would storm through breaches in the walls, their arms furiously swinging two-handed broadswords and battle-axes, or charging forward with long, sharp pikes in front of them. Hot sand, boiling water, and rocks rained down upon the attackers, adding to the chaos and confusion. High up on the ramparts, the castle's commander would order his archers to cut loose a deadly metal cloud of iron-tipped arrows, raining them down on the luckless attackers below. Such were the actions of desperate men in a siege, knowing full well their lives would be cut short by a single, wicked slice of hard, cold steel unless they could stop their opponents by doing the same to them first. How similar this was to a pitched battle, yet made even worse in that there was no escape, no place to retreat!

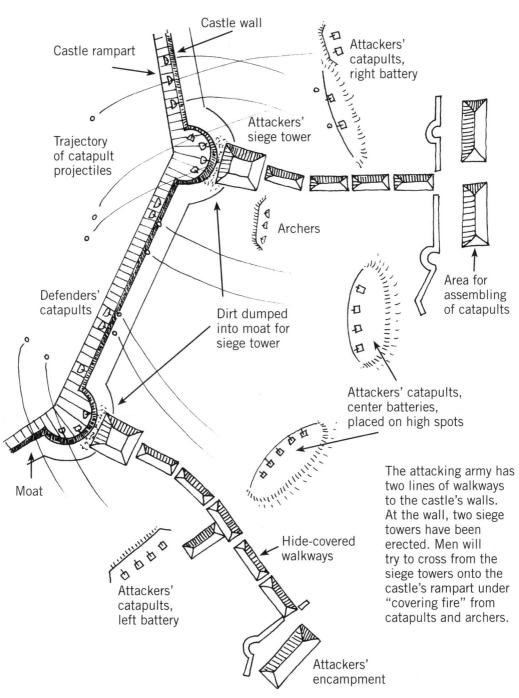

Castle wall

Castle rampart

Attackers' catapults, right battery

Trajectory of catapult projectiles

Attackers' siege tower

Archers

Defenders' catapults

Dirt dumped into moat for siege tower

Area for assembling of catapults

Moat

Attackers' catapults, center batteries, placed on high spots

The attacking army has two lines of walkways to the castle's walls. At the wall, two siege towers have been erected. Men will try to cross from the siege towers onto the castle's rampart under "covering fire" from catapults and archers.

Hide-covered walkways

Attackers' catapults, left battery

Attackers' encampment

2.7 A bird's-eye view of a siege.

CATAPULTS AROUND THE WORLD

Stories of catapults first appear in ancient Greek manuscripts. Writers and historians such as Heron of Alexandria, Ctesibius, and Philon of Byzantium provided several detailed accounts of catapults and directions for building them in their manuscripts. Later on, several Roman writers left us with excellent descriptions of their catapult artillery, perhaps most importantly the famous architect and master of the Roman Emperor Augustus's siege engines, Vitruvius. In fact, there are records and descriptions from all over the world—China, India, the Middle East, and Europe.

Catapults changed greatly in their appearance and construction from the time they were first used in 400 BCE to when they were finally displaced by gunpowder cannons nearly 2,000 years later. During this long period of ancient and medieval history, catapults represented the most advanced and sophisticated application of mechanical engineering knowledge practiced. They were by far the largest, most complex, and most costly mechanical devices in the world.

Not surprisingly, given their lengthy and widespread history, different writers at different times used diverse names to refer to the

17

same types of catapults. So, the machine that the Greeks might term a ballista, the Romans might call a tormentum; the one that the English might term a trebuchet, a Scandinavian might describe as a blida. The machine that the medieval French might term a perrier, the Seljuk Turks might call al-manajaniq. Even in the same country, people called the same catapults different things. All the various names are confusing. The only thing that's certain is this—the same basic catapult might have different names depending upon who is describing it.

To reduce the confusion, this book will define and describe key types of catapults and stick with those definitions throughout this book. This is not to say that these definitions are final or universally agreed upon by scholars. The great number of catapult types and the number of names they had make that impossible.

CATAPULT NAMES

In general, we'll call any mechanical device built for the purposes of hurling missiles (rocks, arrows, or anything else desired to be hurled through the air at an enemy) by the general term "catapult."

But this is a very broad term, so it is helpful to subdivide catapults according to how they are powered.

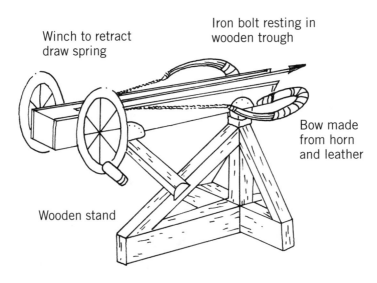

3.1 Greek-style tension catapult, approximately 350 BCE.

Tension Catapults

The earliest catapults built by the Greeks were much like very large bows and arrows. They shot short, heavy darts called "bolts." They were powerful, but they were big and heavy and took a long time to load and fire. In general, these early catapults obtained their shooting power from bending back a wooden or animal-horn bow or leaf spring. Such weapons were called tension catapults. It was the tension in the fibers of the bow that provided the motive force.

Other names for tension catapults included gastrophetes, oxybeles, l'espringale, and the spring engine.

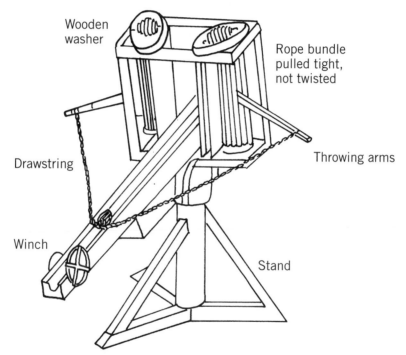

Wooden washer

Rope bundle pulled tight, not twisted

Drawstring

Throwing arms

Winch

Stand

3.2 Greek rock thrower torsion catapult, approximately 325 BCE.

Torsion Catapults

In the third century BCE, the Greeks started to experiment with different types of springs to shoot the bolts, and they came up with the idea of using tightly strung coils of rope. This worked well, since the spring could be made very large and powerful by simply coiling the rope many times over.

Engineers call a spring made this way a "torsion spring," and so catapults powered by coiled ropes are called torsion catapults.

There are many Greek, Roman, European, and Middle Eastern names for torsion catapults. Chiroballista, arcuballista, onager, scorpion, mangonel, stone thrower, and lithobolos are a few of the many names given to torsion-powered catapults.

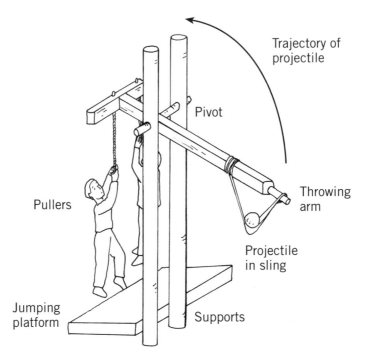

3.3 Early Chinese traction catapult, approximately 200 CE.

Traction Catapults

The next change in catapult technology was the use of human power to shoot rocks. The ancient catapult engineers designed lever-based machines that were fast operating and accurate. When the operator pulled down hard on a lever, the machine could hurl a rock much larger and farther than one could be thrown by an unaided soldier's arm.

Traction catapults were often just called by the generic term "traction catapult," but sometimes were called pull-thrower, hsuan feng (by the Chinese), or witches' hair (in the Near East).

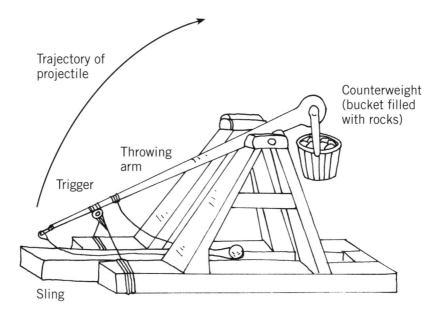

Trajectory of projectile

Counterweight (bucket filled with rocks)

Throwing arm

Trigger

Sling

3.4 European gravity catapult (trebuchet), approximately 1250 CE.

Gravity Catapults

The last type of catapult to be invented was the gravity-powered catapult. These machines used very heavy weights to flip a lever arm to which a rock was attached. When the weight fell, it tossed the ammunition toward the enemy castle in a high, soaring arc. These machines were called trebuchets in general, but had other names, such as couillard, petrary, bricole, and blida.

These gravity-powered catapults were the biggest of all the catapults and, just like battleships, were often given their own names. We can read of very large catapults with names such as the Bull Slinger, the Queen, the Wild Cat, the Parson, and the Bad Neighbor.

A CATAPULT BY ANY OTHER NAME

Scholars and historians have studied catapults for many years, because by understanding them they could better comprehend the conduct and consequences of classical and medieval wars. And, indeed, much has been written about them.

We have very good descriptions of the catapults used by the ancient Greeks. Several Greek historians wrote down extremely detailed descriptions of their throwing machines. Men like Heron of Alexandria, Biton of Greece, and Philon of Byzantium left us with excellent records of ancient Greek hurling machines.

The different types of catapults were each named by the country or even the writer recording the history of their use. The French might call their machines engines à verge (engines of siege), while the Italians might call the same device mangana, and the Vikings might call theirs blida. As we said before, the only certain thing is that catapults certainly went by a lot of different names!

While other writers and historians may differ in the terms they use, here are the names we'll use in this book to describe our catapults and what they are:

Catapult and Siege Engine—Generic terms used to describe all the machines that hurled projectiles before the invention of gunpowder

Spring Engine—a machine that shot missiles powered by a flat or leaf spring

Onager—Roman-style catapult powered by a single horizontal torsion spring

Ballista—Greek-style catapult powered by a double vertical torsion spring

Traction Catapult—a human-powered catapult, operated by men pulling on ropes

Trebuchet—a gravity-powered catapult operated by a heavy counterweight

THE EVOLUTION OF CATAPULTS

Why did catapults change from spring-powered dart and stone throwers to big gravity-powered rock hurlers? There are a lot of different theories that attempt to answer this question.

Many authorities believe that the spring-powered artillery of the Greeks and Romans often didn't work too well in bad weather. If the weather was wet, then the rope bundles—which were made from vegetable fibers or hair or cattle sinews—would stretch. When that happened, the catapults lost most of their throwing power. It was the springiness in the tightly wound coils of rope that gave the machine the ability to throw, and if the rope stretched, well, it just couldn't throw with any sort of real power. That's why historians find lots of references in books and pictures of spring-powered ballistae and man-gonels in use in places like sunny Greece, Spain, and the Levant (the coastal areas where modern Turkey, Lebanon, and Israel are now), but barely a word if anything at all about them being used in wet, damp England or northern France.

Around 1100 CE a new type of stone thrower, and an important one at that, came to Europe by way of China and the Middle East. It was made out of a stout swinging beam that pivoted horizontally, with a sling at the shooting end and ropes at the other that were pulled simultaneously by a gang of men. When a man, or two or three pulled on the rope simultaneously they could toss a rock a very long distance. If 10 or 20 men all pulled simultaneously, they could throw a boulder large enough to knock down a heavy, thick door. This type of catapult, the traction catapult, worked no matter what the weather—hot, cold, sunny, or wet. It was an artillery piece for all seasons. Besides that, a traction-style catapult could be loaded and fired at a much faster rate than spring-type catapults. With a spring-powered (or torsion-powered) catapult, the operators had to load a rock into the sling, "cock" or pull back the cross arms with a big winch, lock the arms in firing position, and then pull the trigger. This took quite a bit of time.

With the traction catapult, it was just a matter of loading it up with a rock and pulling on the ropes. Load and pull, load and pull—fast! For these two reasons, all-weather capability and speed of fire, the traction catapults replaced the old-fashioned torsion catapults speedily. So traction catapults were the best bang for the buck all over Europe, used with tremendous success in various sieges and crusades, until about the year 1200. Around that time, some nameless Arabian or European engineer got a look at the Chinese style of trebuchet. He probably asked himself this question: "Instead of having a host of big, strong men pulling on ropes, why don't we do what the Chinese do and simply attach a great counterweight to the end of the lever?" If the master of engines did this, why, then he needed fewer men to work the device. Besides that, to throw a bigger rock, all he needed to do was to increase the size of the counterweight. And, even better, such machines were very, very accurate, since the pulling power was always the same for any particular weight. With men pulling, sometimes they might pull harder than other times and the projectile could go farther or shorter than the master wanted.

For all these reasons, catapult technology took another leap forward, and great counterweights were substituted for the gang of men who pulled the ropes. These big counterweighted machines were called trebuchets, and some really, really big machines were developed around the start of the thirteenth century.

Now, because the counterweight made the firing of a trebuchet so repeatable and so accurate, a well-commanded catapult team using good, round, stone balls of equal weight could hit the exact same spot on a castle wall with each and every shot. Even a stone wall made from hunks of sandstone twelve feet thick would eventually crumble under a constant barrage of trebuchet stones.

How fast could a trebuchet fire? We have historical records that tell us a big trebuchet, designed by Bishop Durand of Albi, was used to besiege the stronghold of Montsegur in Italy during a religious war called the Albigensian Crusade in the year 1244. The fortress of Montsegur had rock walls many feet thick. It stood high atop a solid rock outcrop. It had a strong and commanding position over any besieging army who felt brave or foolish enough to try and attack it. But even with all these advantages, the castle still fell to the Crusaders, because of the power and accuracy of their big trebuchet. Durand's trebuchet threw rocks, some weighing as much as 175 pounds, at its walls at 20-minute intervals, day and night, for weeks on end. Finally, the onslaught opened holes in the castle walls that allowed the fanatical crusaders to enter the fortress and thus doomed the religious "heretics" hiding inside.

One of the reasons catapults were such effective weapons is that they were extremely versatile in terms of what they could shoot. While large rocks were certainly the favorite projectiles for demolishing castle walls, catapults could be designed with many different sorts of baskets, slings, and pouches. A siege engine could be designed to hurl just about any type of projectile that the engine commander chose to shoot.

What kinds of projectiles did catapults throw? There were a great variety of objects used for ammunition. Since it was easy to throw almost anything from the sling of a trebuchet or the basket of an onager, ancient artillery men would choose whatever they thought would be most effective against their enemy.

For example, if the plan was to knock down castle walls, then large, heavy stones were preferred. The stones would be shaped into regular round balls of approximately equal size and weight so they could be aimed reliably. If the artillery unit needed to attack wooden buildings or palisades (a palisade is a wooden fence surrounding a fort), then they would often hurl barrels made of thin wooden slats filled with a burning liquid. The barrels would break against the fence and set it aflame.

In fact, almost every heavy, hard, unpleasant, or disgusting object that you could think of was used in catapult attacks. There are records showing and describing many different types of ammunition:
- Rocks
- Carved stone balls
- Iron arrows
- Lead shot
- Baskets of venomous snakes
- Diseased horse carcasses
- Clay pots filled with asphyxiating gas
- Flaming barrels of gooey, syrupy chemicals
- Hornet's nests
- The dead bodies of captured enemy soldiers
- The severed heads of messengers
- Cattle manure

There was almost no limit to the creativity of ancient fighters when it came to selecting ammunition. There are historical accounts of 2,000 full cartloads of animal manure being thrown at the siege of Carolstein by Lithuanian attackers in the late Middle Ages. Edward I of England was fond of gigantic carved stone boulders. But probably the most fearsome thing ever to be hurled by catapults was flaming barrels of liquid fire.

As far back as 600 BCE incendiary mixtures were used in warfare. Various concoctions were mixed together and hurled over the walls and gates of enemy fortifications. The ingredients in such mixtures included sulfur, pitch, sawdust, and oils of various types and weights. The formulation of incendiary compounds was somewhat akin to making homemade chili—everyone had their own secret ingredients for making it better. Some ingredients made it stickier, some made it burn more intensely, and others made the fire harder to extinguish.

How all these additives helped is hard to determine. For instance, adding sulfur gave the mixture a horrible smell. Other ingredients, such as rock salts, made the fire glow bright orange. Medieval recipes for incendiary compositions included such unusual ingredients as oil of benedict (made by soaking bricks in olive oil), saracolle (a tree resin collected only in Ethiopia), and crabapple juice.

To use incendiary ammunition, the master of engines would have his men mix large batches of flammable, foul-smelling goop in giant wooden tubs. Then they would fill thin-walled barrels with the compound, set it afire, and use catapults to hurl them over enemy castle walls and into towns.

Of all the fiery substances shot from catapults, the one used by the Byzantines was the best known. It was called Greek fire, because it was the Byzantine Greek armies that first used it. The ingredients in the recipe for Greek fire are no longer known with certainty, but they likely included sulfur, tree resins like tar and pitch, asphalt, petroleum, vegetable oil, manure, turpentine, and powdered lime. Sometimes rags soaked in Greek fire were attached to arrows and shot by archers.

Speeding, sharp, and sometimes flaming arrows were among the most effective types of projectiles. And, in medieval times, some inventors were able to devise machines that could flood an area with arrows. Such a device was the spring engine, an arrow-shooting artillery device that used a wooden spring to shower arrows over an entire battlefield.

Wild Donkey:
An Onager Catapult

Adult supervision required

Use protective eyewear

 Swinging arm alert: watch out for moving arms or levers

Sharp and/or heavy tool advisory: Project requires use of saw or hammer

Flying object alert: Use care when aiming and firing

The onager-style catapult was among the most successful catapult designs ever created. Powerful, easy to make, and accurate, it had many advantages. The Roman historian Ammianus Marcellius, who lived around the year 350 BCE, wrote much about Roman army life as he personally experienced it when he was a Roman soldier. Here is his description of the type of catapult that the Romans called the Wild Donkey, or onager.

10.6

A[n] Onager's framework is made out of two oak beams, straight except for a hump in the middle. There are large holes in the middle of each beam, through which strong ropes made from cattle sinews are stretched and twisted. A long arm is inserted between the bundles of rope. At the end of the arm is [a] pouch for holding the projectile and a pin. When the pin is released, the arm rotates until it strikes a crossarm covered with a sack stuffed with fine chaff and secured by tight binding.

During combat, a round stone is placed in the pouch and the arm is winched down. Then, the master artillery-man strikes the pin with a hammer, and with a big blow, the stone is launched towards the target.

It was not only the ancient Greeks and Romans who built and used the onager. This weapon was popular with the armies of a large number of tribes and nations. Records are sketchy, but it was probably used for a very long time. The onager was a simple yet effective weapon and was used long after the more complex types of ballistae designed by the Greeks were forgotten. It is possible that catapults of this sort, with a single horizontally mounted rope spring and cloth sling, were used well into the Middle Ages.

MATERIALS

- Saw
- Drill
- ½-inch drill bit
- ⅛-inch drill bit
- ³⁄₁₆-inch drill bit
- Ball peen hammer
- 1-inch-long nails
- Glue
- Small hook and eye
- Sandpaper

THE CATAPULT FRAME

- (2) 1-inch by 1-inch by 10-inch pieces of pine (Frame) You can find the wood pieces in the dowel section of most hardware and home stores
- (2) 1-inch by 1-inch by 4-inch pieces of pine (Uprights)
- (3) 1-inch by 1-inch by 4-inch pieces of pine (Cross Members)
- (2) ¾-inch by ¾-inch by 4-inch pieces of pine (Upright Supports)
- (4) 1-inch by 1-inch by 2-inch pieces of pine (Footers)
- (4) 2-inch-diameter wheels
- (4) 1½-inch axles to fit wheels

THE TORSION SPRING AND THROWING ARM ASSEMBLY

- (1) ⅝-inch wooden dowel, 8½ inches long (Throwing Arm)
- (1) 18-inch length of ⅛-inch nylon cord
- (2) ½-inch-diameter washers
- (4) ³⁄₁₆-inch-diameter dowels, 1½ inches long
- (1) #10 machine screw, ½ inch long, with corresponding nut and lock washer
- (1) 2-inch-diameter fender washer, with a small diameter inside hole

DIRECTIONS

General Notes

1. It is important to cut all of the wooden pieces to the sizes shown as accurately and as squarely as possible. Sand each piece after cutting to smooth it and remove splinters.
2. Wooden pieces may be attached to one another by using nails, glue, wooden dowels, or any combination thereof. If you want a sturdier model catapult, then use wooden dowels instead of nails to connect the parts.

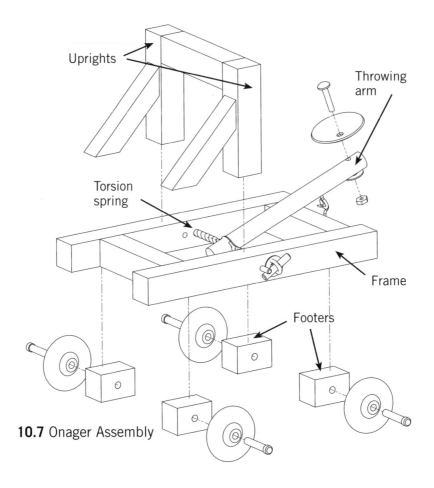

10.7 Onager Assembly

3. A picture is worth a thousand words, so refer to the assembly diagrams throughout to understand how all the subassemblies are made. The exploded **diagram 10.7** shows how all the parts will eventually fit together in the completed project.

Building the Onager Frame, Uprights, and Footings

1. Drill a ³⁄₁₆-inch-diameter hole in the two Frame pieces at a point 5 inches from-one end.
2. Drill a ½-inch-diameter hole in the Frame pieces at a point ½ inch from the same end.

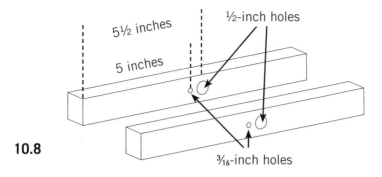

5½ inches

½-inch holes

5 inches

10.8

¾₁₆-inch holes

3. Drill a hole the same size as the wheel axles you have (often, but not always ⁵⁄₁₆-inch diameter) in the center of each of the four Footers.

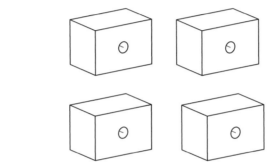

10.9

4. Attach the two Cross Members to the Frame pieces as shown in **diagram 10.10**, using glue and/or nails, or dowels.

Cross members

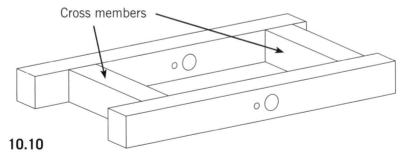

10.10

5. Attach the two Uprights to the Frame, using glue and/or nails, or dowels. Connect the top ends of the Uprights with the third Cross Member.

6. Cut 45-degree angles on the ends of the Upright Support pieces so they form trapezoidal shaped pieces as in **diagram 10.11**.

Attach the two Upright Supports to the framework, one end to the Frame piece and the other to the Uprights. The Upright Supports brace the upper Cross Member so it can withstand the impact of the Throwing Arm.

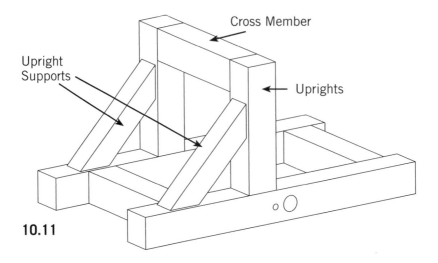

10.11

7. Attach all the Footers to the framework as shown in **diagram 10.7** using glue and/or nails.
8. Insert the Wheels and Axles.

BUILDING THE THROWING ARM

1. Attach the eyehook to the Throwing Arm, and the hook to the rear Cross Member. They must align so that the hook mates with the eyehook when the arm is retracted.

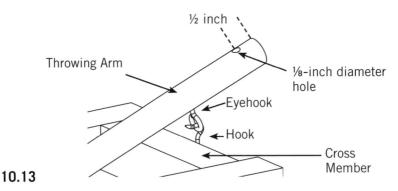

10.13

2. Drill a ⅛-inch-diameter hole in the Throwing Arm, ½ inch from the end, as shown in **diagram 10.12**.

3. With the round end of a ball peen hammer, shape the fender washer into a cup.

4. Attach the washer, cup side out, to the Throwing Arm with the bolt, lock washer, and nut.

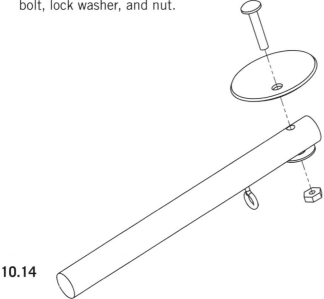

10.14

ASSEMBLING THE TORSION SPRING

1. Tie the cord ends together securely.
2. Insert the looped ends through each ½-inch hole in the Frame. Insert the ³⁄₁₆-inch dowel in each end of the cord on the outboard side of the Frame. **Diagram 10.15** shows a view looking down from above.

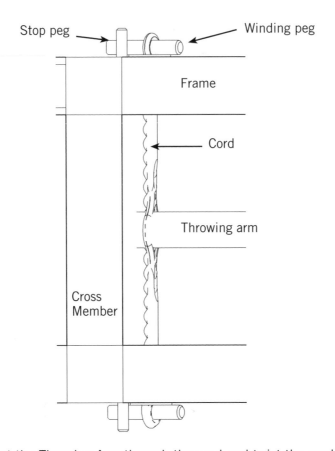

Stop peg — Winding peg
Frame
Cord
Throwing arm
Cross Member

10.15

3. Insert the Throwing Arm through the cord and twist the cord in the direction of the upper Cross Member. (When the cord is twisted, the Throwing Arm will want to pop up, toward the Cross Member.) Tighten the rope spring by turning the pegs a few twists at a time, alternating sides. Continue to twist the cord until it is very tight.

4. When tight, maintain tension in the cord by inserting the stop pegs in the 3/16-inch diameter holes on the Frame pieces.

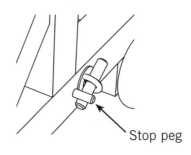

10.16

Stop peg

OPERATING THE ONAGER

1. Carefully pull the Throwing Arm back. Latch with the hook and eye.
2. Place a projectile (such as a walnut) in the cup-shaped washer.
3. Attach a string to the hook. Grab the string and jerk the hook from the eyehook to fire the catapult. The more tension you put in the torsion bundle (the twisted cord), the farther the catapult will shoot.

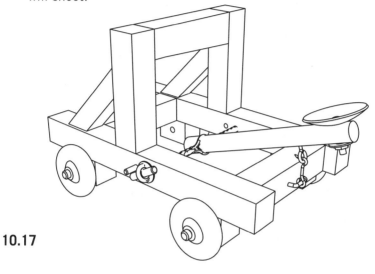

10.17

Viking Catapult

Adult supervision required

Use protective eyewear

Flying object alert: Use care when aiming and firing

The Viking Catapult is an easy-to-make device. Like other tension-powered catapults, it uses the energy stored in the fibers of a resilient material. But instead of using a flexible bow and stiff drawstring, this Viking Catapult uses elastic rubber tubing for energy storage.

Written accounts by monks and historians who lived in the latter half of the first millennium (500 to 1000 BCE) tell of frequent attacks on English and French towns by Viking raiders. When they sailed in on their famous wooden ships, they caused all sorts of trouble for the villagers and town dwellers. The Vikings were infamous for their predilection for sacking and looting. One historical record, written by the French monk Odo in the late ninth century, states that the Vikings did indeed use catapults to storm the gates and walls protecting Paris. No drawings or examples of Viking catapults exist, but there is a great deal known about the way they built other large projects such as ships and wagons. So we can speculate that they built their siege engines in a similar way: with round poles, broad timbers, and sturdy, roped connections.

Basically, the Viking Catapult is made from elastic rubber tubing stretched between a lashed framework of sticks. To use it, you will place a water balloon or similar object in the pouch. Draw back the pouch, release it, and whoosh, the balloon flies downfield. This is a relatively easy project as the whole device is made up of only a few parts. However, it will take some experimentation to achieve the proper tension in the rubber tubing: too much and it will be hard to retract; too little, and your projectiles won't fly very far.

Pay special attention to safety. Don't overextend the tube and don't aim it at people. Hitting a person with a water balloon can be dangerous.

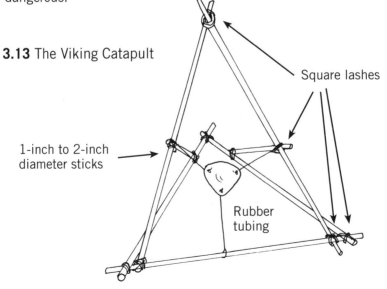

3.13 The Viking Catapult

Square lashes

1-inch to 2-inch diameter sticks

Rubber tubing

MATERIALS

- (1) 9-foot length of $\frac{3}{32}$-inch thick sidewall elastic rubber tubing (Tubing like this is available at good hardware stores, large home stores, and medical supply companies. It is generally sold by the foot.)
- (5) 4-foot-long sticks, approximately 1½ inches to 2 inches in diameter (Note: unlike most of the other projects in this book, the lengths and widths of the parts do not need to be exact; any strong stick approximately 4 to 6 feet long will do nicely—hiking sticks work well, but any strong, straight stick will be adequate. Be sure to choose a stick that is strong enough to support the weights and stresses the catapult puts on it. Some kinds of wood are strong and springy and a thin one will do. Some woods are weak and brittle, so you'll need a thicker one. Choose carefully!)
- (2) 2-foot-long sticks, similar in strength to those above
- 100 feet of ⅛-inch manila rope
- (1) medium-sized, strong, rigid plastic bowl
- Duct or vinyl tape
- Scissors
- Ammunition (water balloons, racquet balls, or other similar items)

A NOTE ON LASHING

This catapult makes use of a construction technique called "lashing." Lashing is the practice of joining wooden sticks or poles together using rope joints. To lash together sticks into a secure joint, follow the basic steps outlined below. Lashing is enjoyable to learn and a useful skill that is often taught in organizations like the Boy Scouts. There is much technique and skill involved in mastering it, but the simple and basic square lash technique is not difficult to learn.

First, learn to tie the knot called the "clove hitch." The clove hitch is the knot you tie to first join the rope to the stick. Directions for tying the clove hitch are shown in **diagram 3.14**.

Step 2   Step 1

3.14 How to Tie a Clove Hitch

Next, **diagram 3.15** shows the basic steps in lashing together two sticks using a square lash. All of the wooden sticks that make up the Viking Catapult are connected using the square lash.

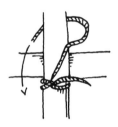 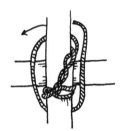 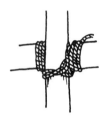

Step 1
Start with a clove hitch, then wrap the loose end around the back, as shown, to form a square.

Step 2
Wrap the rope around the back a second time.

Step 3
Continue to wrap in the same direction three more times.

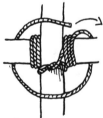 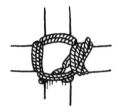

Step 5
After three wraps in the opposite direction, tie off the loose end.

Step 4
Changing direction, wrap the rope back around the back in the opposite direction, called "frapping," as shown.

3.15 How to Tie a Square Lash

Lashing techniques consist of three basic operations: the placement of the sticks, wrapping them, and then "frapping" them (see **diagram 3.15**, Step 4). In order to be successful, here are a few more tips:

- Use manila rope. You can probably be successful using nylon, polypropylene, or even cotton rope, but manila hemp rope is the best for lashing projects. Also, it is more similar to the fibrous twine that the Vikings most likely used.
- Tie your wraps and fraps tightly and securely. This will provide a sturdy structure.

DIRECTIONS

Making the Framework

1. First, assemble the bottom triangle of the catapult framework. Lash together three 4-foot sticks to form an equilateral triangle (one with three equally long sides).
2. Next, lash two more 4-foot sticks to the bottom front corners so that it forms another triangle, pointing up. This will be the triangle to which the rubber tubing will be attached.

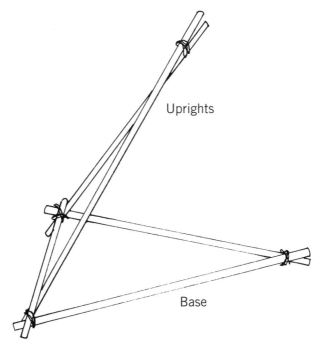

Uprights

Base

3.16

3. Now, set the angle of the triangle of sticks you just made by attaching two 2-foot sticks to the middle of the upright triangle and the back of the bottom triangle. Compare it to **diagram 3.17** below. Note that the triangle of sticks that supports the rubber tubing should be tilted back from vertical. You can vary the angle easily simply by moving the locations of the lashing points back and forth.

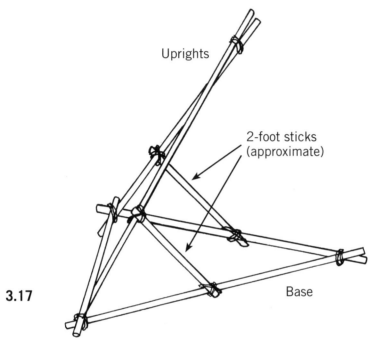

Uprights

2-foot sticks
(approximate)

3.17

Base

4. Cut the rubber tubing into three 3-foot lengths.
5. Drill, cut, or poke three holes in the ammunition holder (a plastic bowl or something similar) and thread the rubber tube through the bowl and the frame as shown in the diagram. Tie knots in the tubing to anchor it in place with tape.

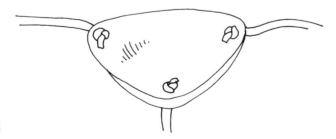

3.18

6. Attach the ammunition holder and rubber tubing to the frame. Use knots to tie together the rubber tubing ends, and be sure to tie the ends of the tubing together using a square knot with at least 1 inch of tubing extending beyond the knot. It is very important that you use a secure knot like a square knot and that you tie in such a fashion that it doesn't come loose. Once the knot is tied, tape it in so the ends are held securely.

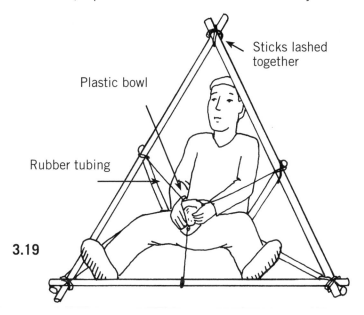

Sticks lashed together

Plastic bowl

Rubber tubing

3.19

OPERATING THE VIKING CATAPULT

1. To operate the Viking Catapult, place ammo in the plastic bowl. Pull back on the bowl and release it.
2. After observing the flight of your ammo, "tune" the rubber tubes in order to make them pull with equal force. Do this by adjusting the position of the knot that holds the tubes to the bowl.

KEEPING SAFETY IN MIND

1. Make sure all knots, including those in the tubing, are tight and secure. Check the knots before putting lots of tension on them.
2. Check the rubber tubing for nicks and wear each time before you shoot. If your catapult becomes worn, replace or repair those parts before using it again.

3. Don't aim at people. Make sure the area downrange is clear of people and other hazards. Keep non-participants out of the area in which you're working.
4. Don't overextend the rubber tubing.
5. Wear safety glasses to protect yourself in the unlikely event the tubing breaks, or knots become untied.

SHOOTING SNAKES IN A BARREL

THE CATAPULTS OF ALEXANDER THE GREAT

Alexander the Great was born in 356 BCE in Macedonia, a part of northern Greece where the modern-day city of Thessaloniki is located. His father was Philip II, a great ruler in his own right, and his mother was Philip's queen, the fair-skinned and red-haired Olympias. Philip was the king of the Macedonians, a warlike people who lived north of the mountains that separated the sophisticated and rich Greek city-states of Athens, Corinth, and Thebes from the semi-barbarians beyond.

Philip was an energetic ruler and a brilliant general. And he was ambitious as well. Philip's goal was to be the ruler of the entire Greek peninsula, and he started wars and precipitated battles with even the most powerful Greek city-states towards this end. Philip's son, Alexander, was like his father: very bright and very aggressive. But Olympias made certain her son was well educated, too, and hired the famous philosopher Aristotle to be his personal tutor. Perhaps due to Aristotle's able teaching, Alexander became fascinated by science, and in particular the science of making war. No kings prior to Philip and Alexander knew as much or cared as much about the machines of warfare.

Catapult warfare was in its infancy, the current state-of-the-art being the cumbersome and somewhat slow-firing gastrophetes weapon.

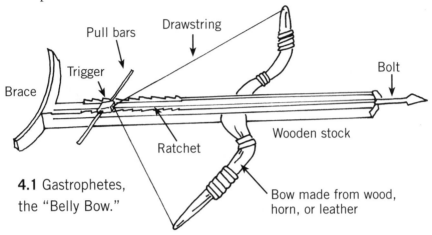

4.1 Gastrophetes, the "Belly Bow."

Many scholars credit now-unknown individuals who lived in the powerful Greek city-states just before the time of King Philip with developing one of the first ancient artillery devices. This device, called the belly-bow or gastrophetes, first appeared in the fifth century BCE. In many ways, this device resembled an oversized crossbow. It was much like a normal bow and arrow except that the bow was extremely stiff—so stiff, in fact, that the user had to brace the end of the device against his stomach, and then retract the drawstring using both hands. Since the pull of the bow was so great, the user couldn't simply release the drawstring as is done on a normal bow and arrow; there was a trigger mechanism that allowed the user to "cock" the device and fire it by releasing a lever.

This device was heavy and crude, and it took a very long time to load and fire. So it wasn't terribly effective except in the case of a long, drawn-out siege, perhaps when hitting a particular stationary target was desired.

Then, around 400 BCE, Dionysius the Elder came up with a great new idea in terms of military technology. Dionysius was the Tyrant of Syracuse, one of the most powerful cities in the entire ancient world.

(In those days "Tyrant" just meant "boss" or "leader" and didn't necessarily mean a ruler was particularly mean or cruel.) He thought he could make his city more powerful and mightier than those of his neighbors by using brains, not just brawn. So instead of going out and hiring mercenary soldiers to fight for Syracuse, as did the other rich and powerful city-states, he did something different and never before attempted: he went out and hired military engineers and scientists. He hired the best and smartest people he could find from Italy, Greece, and Carthage, and the work of these engineers revolutionized their world. Because of their efforts, ancient Syracuse had the best warships, the best armor, the best fortresses, and now, the best weapons.

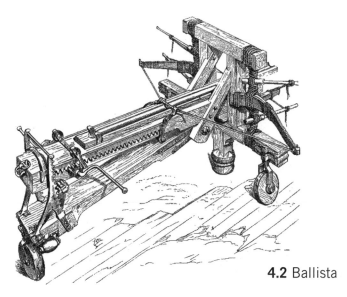

4.2 Ballista

In 399 BCE Dionysius besieged a walled town called Motya that was located on the island of Sicily. It was a long and bitter siege. The Syracuseans brought their ships very close, drawing them up on the beaches outside the town. The Syracuseans surrounded the town. According to the Greek historian Diodorus, the Motyans counterattacked the Syracuseans but "were held back by a great quantity of flying missiles. The Syracuseans slew many of the enemy by using from the land the catapults which shot sharp pointed missiles. Indeed, this weapon caused great dismay, because it was a new invention at the time."

And so the first instance of any type of artillery battle in history is recorded. The Syracuseans routed the Motyans and started to massacre them, but finally they relented because they wanted to capture those who remained alive to sell for slaves.

Dionysius and this military think tank may have come up with the idea of mounted catapults, but it was the Macedonians in general and Alexander the Great in particular who took catapult warfare to a whole new level, leading to the development of the large, free-standing, and powerful bolt and arrow shooters now known as "ballistae." Engineers working for Philip II of Macedonia, father of Alexander the Great, most likely first invented the ballista; and engineers of Alexander, perhaps under his personal direction, perfected it. Initially it was simply an improvement of Dionysius's oversized slingshot, using the springiness of a bow (as in a bow and arrow) fabricated from animal parts, like horns and cartilage, as well as wood. As at the Siege of Motya, such devices worked reasonably well, but soon Alexander's catapult engineers had gone as far as they could in terms of getting distance and power out of a bow composed of wood and animal parts. So they came up with a new idea.

Instead of using the limited energy storage capacity coming from the tension in a bent bow, why not, they thought, use springs made from tightly strung coils of rope? When you twist a rope tightly, the rope resists the rotation and pushes back in the opposite direction. So, if you made a bundle of big, strong, tightly strung rope coils, they could store and then release a lot of energy. And the bigger and more tightly tensioned you made the rope bundle, the more energy it stored, the bigger the projectile it could throw, and the longer that projectile would fly.

The Greeks named this device, one of the first torsion catapults, "the lithobolos." It used two vertical bundles of rope made from hair or animal tendons that were strung tight like the strings on a tennis racket to form a powerful spring. A spring that gets its power from storing energy via a twisting motion is called a torsion spring, so this kind of catapult is called a torsion catapult.

Wooden throwing arms were inserted in between the ropes that made up the catapult spring. An arrow-holding sling was attached to the free ends of both arms and then retracted back against the force of the rope spring, in a fashion similar to an archer pulling back the drawstring of a bow. Because of the power of the torsion spring, a winch or windlass was necessary to retract the drawstring and sling. A short, heavy, iron-tipped dart was placed in a sling on the cord. When the sling was released, the twisted ropes pulled hard, very hard, shot the wooden arms forward, and hurled the spear toward the enemy with enormous force and reasonable accuracy.

ALEXANDER OF MACEDONIA

In 336 BCE King Philip was killed under mysterious circumstances, and Alexander ascended to the throne of Macedonia. Alexander came into his own as a great leader and general. No leader had ever come close to accomplishing what Alexander, his armies, and his catapults accomplished. Within 12 years Alexander had conquered city after city, state after state. By the time he died just 13 years later, in 323 BCE, Alexander's rule extended from Greece south to Egypt, and east through Mesopotamia and Persia to as far as India. His kingdom included the area occupied by the present-day countries of Greece, Turkey, Egypt, Iraq, Iran, Syria, Israel, Pakistan, Afghanistan, and parts of India and the Balkans. The area he ruled was nearly as great in size as all of modern Europe.

Certainly, Alexander made good use of the army originally created by his father, but he took the limits of Macedonian and Greek power to levels King Philip could never have imagined.

ALEXANDER ON THE MARCH

Wasting no time after taking the throne, in 334 BCE Alexander and his army started his eastward march of conquest by engaging the ancient and traditional enemies of the Greeks: the Persians. The two armies met for the first time at the Granicus River, in Asia Minor (in present-day Turkey). Alexander and 40,000 men charged the attacking Persians. Charge followed countercharge, during which the rocks and arrows shot from ballistae rained down on the battlefield like

47

hailstones in a strong spring storm. The attack continued until the Persian line of defense on the river crumbled and they turned and fled. All that stood between Alexander and total victory was a force of tough, disciplined Greek mercenaries, soldiers paid by the Persians to fight for them. A climactic battle between the Persians and the Macedonians raged, both sides fighting with a fanatical ardor. A courageous charge by Alexander and his Macedonian phalanx (a battle formation in which soldiers lock shields and expose only a bristling array of long spears to the enemy) finally routed the mercenaries, and Alexander emerged victorious, leaving the Persian forces wildly retreating and battered.

THE SIEGE OF TYRE

After Alexander had defeated the Persians at the River Granicus, he continued his march eastward and engaged the Persians, under their leader Darius, for the second time at the mountain town of Issus. Again, Alexander soundly defeated the Persians and continued south down the Levantine coast (the eastern Mediterranean coastline of Lebanon and Israel), for his plan was to gain control over the entire eastern Mediterranean coast from Greece all around to Egypt. He went westward and then moved southward down the seacoast, and the cities of Sidon and Byblos surrendered to him without a fight.

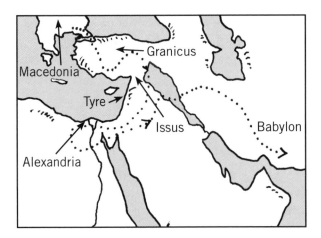

4.3 A map of Alexander's march through Tyre.

Continuing to the south, he came upon the great island city of Tyre in 332 BCE. Initially, relations between Tyre and Alexander were cordial. But then the Tyrian rulers angered Alexander by refusing to let him enter the city to worship the Greek god Herakles in their temple. Matters escalated beyond the point where words could be of further use, and so began the famous Siege of Tyre.

Tyre was an island fortress off the coast of modern Lebanon. It was located in the Mediterranean Sea about half a mile from the mainland, separated from the coast by a fairly shallow channel of water that ranged from 5 to 10 feet deep. The Tyrians had surrounded their city with huge stone walls, 150 feet high in places, a well-fortified harbor, and virtually no land outside the walls from which a siege could be staged. So its citizens, with some justification, thought their fortress city was impregnable.

Sound military strategy dictated that Alexander could not simply bypass this city. He could not leave an unfriendly city, especially one as powerful as Tyre, in a position to rise against him later, possibly in league with the Persians. In order to reach his goal of controlling the entire eastern Mediterranean coast, Tyre simply had to be taken, and so Alexander and his generals made battle plans.

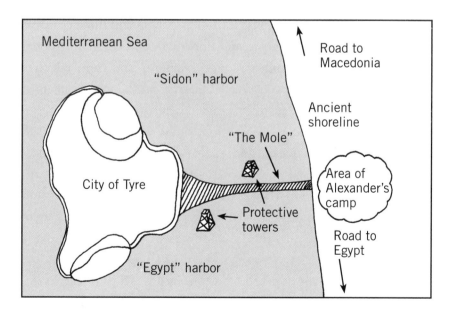

4.4 Map of Tyre.

Now, the Tyrians knew Alexander was coming and had stocked up on supplies; Tyre also had its own source of fresh water within its high walls. It would require extraordinary measures to conquer this town.

To take the city, Alexander decided to build a bridge of earth and boulders, 200 yards wide, from the mainland out into the sea to the walls of the fortress city. This land bridge, which the Greeks termed a "mole," required a span of about half a mile. At first the builders made rapid progress, because they were near the mainland and there were no Tyrians to hinder or attack them with arrows and missiles. But as they began to build farther from the shore, they started to work in deeper water, and simultaneously they came nearer the city itself. The Macedonians had to endure a vigorous attack, being assailed with missiles from the catapults on the city walls. And even worse for Alexander, the Tyrians still retained command of the sea, so they raided the workers building the mole, firing arrows and stones from tiremes (ancient warships powered by oarsmen and sometimes sails), making it impossible for the Macedonians to continue to fill in the earthen bridge.

Few historical figures display the strength of conviction that belonged to Alexander. Once he began a project, Alexander was relentless. He spared no expense on this siege. He had hired many of the best engineers from Cyprus and Phoenicia, and they constructed a vast number of the strongest, longest-ranging, and most effective catapults. Some of these were erected directly on the mole, but most were placed on two high platforms, called siege towers, built on ocean piers alongside the mole. In addition, other catapults were placed shipboard on converted vessels normally used for transporting horses.

The Tyrians erected towers of their own on the fortress walls opposite the mole, and they outfitted those with big stone- and spear-throwing catapults as well. Alexander's biographer, a man named Arrian, tells us that the Tyrian towers were 150 feet high, very wide, and solid, as they were made from layer upon layer of stone. It was not easy for the converted horse-transport ships of the Macedonians, which were conveying the engines of war up to the wall, to approach the city, because a great quantity of stones hurled at them prevented them from getting close enough to fire.

Making things even more difficult for Alexander, the Tyrians, according to contemporary writers, erected a clever contraption never before seen. High atop the fortress walls, they placed a series of enormous spinning wheels, one next to another. When the Macedonians shot rocks at the fortress city with their catapults, the spokes in the spinning wheels high on the walls would intercept the missiles and knock them down. They may have even caught the rocks in mid-air and sent them hurtling back! No one knows exactly what these machines looked like, but several possibilities exist.

Eventually Alexander's ships were able to get close enough to the city walls to attempt an assault. The tension- and torsion- powered catapults on both sides set up a fury of fire-tipped arrows, iron darts, and heavy rocks. The Tyrians grew desperate when they saw Alexander's ships draw close and decided to make a preemptive attack.

This daring daylight raid initially worked well for Tyre, and the strong Tyrian navy sunk several ships caught at anchor without their crews. But once Alexander rallied his troops and his navy, the tide of battle quickly turned. The Macedonian tiremes swung into battle, rowing hard and ramming the enemy ships with their reinforced metal bows. The Macedonian navy had also equipped their ships with maritime catapults, which were used to shoot thin wooden barrels loaded with poisonous snakes onto the decks of the enemy ships.

When the barrels broke on deck and the slithering, venomous serpents crawled out, the Tyrian sailors were absolutely horrified. Imagine the panic, the terror that a sailor must have experienced when a barrel full of agitated and poisonous vipers broke apart at his feet! No doubt this action made more than a few jump overboard in a frantic effort to avoid death by snakebite.

Alexander's soldiers reloaded the catapults, this time with new ammunition: hornet's nests. The angry wasps swarmed over the decks of the enemy ships, buzzing and stinging in a horrible, ancient kind of biological warfare. With such weapons, Alexander could clear the decks of an entire enemy ship with a single well-aimed toss.

4.5 A "spinning wheel" of Tyre.

After the naval battle, the Macedonians had control of the sea, and it was time to finally bring the battering rams to bear against the city's walls. Again and again they slammed the walls, and at last a hole was opened. After a short but intense struggle, Alexander and his troops took the wall and advanced into the main part of the city.

More than 8,000 Tyrians were killed in the final attack, and the remaining 30,000 inhabitants were sold into slavery. The Siege of Tyre had a lasting effect geographically as well as historically: Alexander's mole stayed in place for centuries, causing the sea around it to eventually fill with gravel and silt, and today Tyre is no longer an island; it is part of the mainland. Alexander, in his drive to conquer, permanently changed the face of the Mediterranean. Such deeds account for the fame and legends of Alexander, and he remains famous almost 2,500 years later.

Of Alexander's courage at this siege, another ancient biographer, Roman historian Quinus Curtius Rufus, wrote:

> Alexander climbed the highest siege-tower. His courage was great, for the danger was also great, he being conspicuous in his royal insignia and flashing armor. He was the prime target of enemy missiles thrown by Tyrian catapults. And his actions in the engagement were spectacular. He transfixed with his spear many of the defenders on the walls, and some he threw headlong after striking them in hand-to-hand combat with his sword or shield, for the tower from which he fought practically touched the walls of Tyre.

Alexander's Artillery: The Macedonian Ballista

Adult supervision required

Sharp and/or heavy tool advisory: Project requires use of saw or hammer

Flying object alert: Use care when aiming and firing

Without doubt, catapults played an important role in the military tactics of Alexander and his Macedonian soldiers. The Macedonians built some very elegant and sophisticated siege weapons. Most likely they built and used both torsion-powered and tension-style catapults, capable of hurling darts and perhaps stones.

4.6 Ballista Model

This project shows you how to build a working model Ballista made from wood, much like those designed and built by the Greek engineers of Alexander, used to take the fortress city of Tyre. The Ballista is a torsion-powered machine, and this model uses two coils of twisted rope to transfer energy to the projectile. As you can see, this catapult shoots its ammunition straight and low, like a rifle, unlike the other types of ancient artillery, which are designed to lob missiles in a high looping arc. For that reason, this type of catapult was especially effective against vertical targets like doors and gates.

MATERIALS

- (2) 1-inch by 1-inch by 8-inch wood pieces (Horizontal Spring Frame) You can find 1-by-1 and ½-by-½ wood pieces in the dowel bins at most large hardware and home stores. Unlike "dimensional lumber," dowels are sized exactly.
- (2) 1-inch by 1-inch by 2-inch wood pieces (Outboard Vertical Spring Frame)
- (2) ½-inch by ½-inch by 2-inch wood pieces (Inboard Vertical Spring Frame)
- (4) 1½-inch steel washers
- (4) ³⁄₁₆-inch-diameter by 1-inch wooden dowels (Stop Pegs)
- (4) ³⁄₁₆-inch-diameter by 1-inch wooden dowels (Turning Dowels)
- (2) ⅜-inch-diameter by 5-inch wooden dowels (Throwing Arms)
- (4) ⅛-inch-diameter by 2½-inch wooden dowels (Windlass Turning Pegs)

- (1) ½-inch-diameter by 6½-inch dowel (Windlass Dowel)
- (1) 1-inch by 1-inch by ½-inch wood piece (Horizontal Windlass Frame)
- (2) 1-inch by 1-inch by 2½-inch wood pieces (Vertical Windlass Frame)
- (1) 1-inch by 1-inch by 10-inch wood piece (Bed)
- (1) small hook and eye bolt
- (1) ½-inch by ½-inch by 2⅜-inch wood piece (Pusher)
- (2) 1-inch by 1-inch by 1½-inch wooden pieces (Footer)
- (2) Toy Wheels and Axles
- String or cord for rope springs
- Saw
- Hammer
- Small nails
- Glue
- Drill and drill bits
- Sandpaper

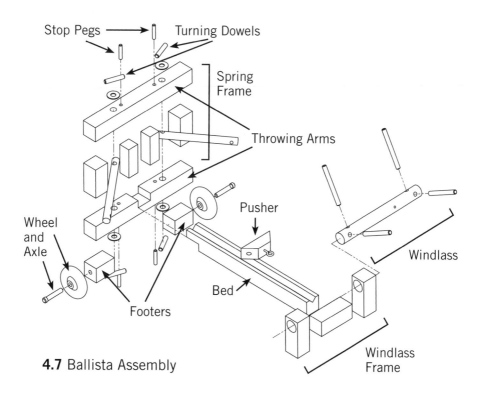

4.7 Ballista Assembly

DIRECTIONS

Take a look at **diagram 4.7**, the Ballista Assembly, to understand how all the parts go together. This sort of drawing is called an "exploded diagram." An exploded diagram is a very useful tool in building models because it shows all of the parts and how they all fit together.

The ancient engineers who first described these machines referred to the spring frame as the "scutula," or hole carrier. Why did they call it this? Because that's just what it was—it was the wooden square with the all-important holes through which the rope spring passed. When the catapult engineers wanted to build a catapult, the very first thing they decided on was how big these holes would be. Once that was decided, they then knew how big the rope spring, the torsion bundle (or as the Romans called it, the "tonus"), would be, and then how thick the wooden framework had to be, and how long and how heavy the bolt could be, and so on. The scutula set the stage for all other dimensions, so the hole carrier was the most important part of all.

1. Drill two ⅜-inch-diameter holes, centered, 2 inches from either end in the Top Horizontal Spring Frame, as shown.

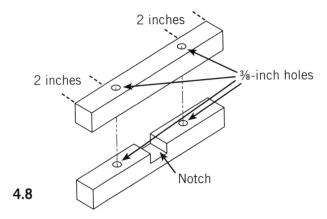

4.8

2. Drill two ⅜-inch-diameter holes, 2 inches from either end in the Bottom Horizontal Spring Frame, as shown above. In addition, cut a 1-inch-wide by ½-inch-deep notch in the center of the piece.

3. Drill a ⅛-inch-diameter hole in each Throwing Arm, ⅜ inches from the end.

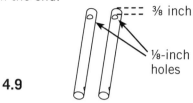

⅜ inch

⅛-inch holes

4.9

4. Drill four ⅛-inch holes through the Windlass Dowel, ½-inch and ½-inch from each end. Each hole should be drilled 90 degrees to the preceding hole. Refer to the diagram below for clarification.

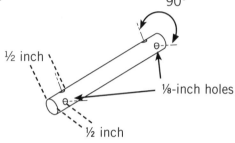

90°

½ inch

⅛-inch holes

4.10

½ inch

5. Cut a 1-inch-long by ½-inch-deep notch in one end of the Bed Piece. This will seat on the notch on Lower Horizontal Spring Frame. File or sand if necessary to obtain a good fit.

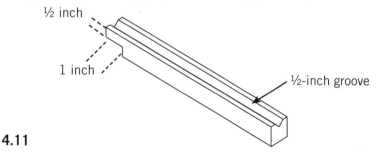

½ inch

1 inch

½-inch groove

4.11

6. Optional: Cut a ½-inch-wide by ½-inch-deep groove in one face of the Bed Piece as shown in **diagram 4.11**.

7. Cut 45-degree angle in the Pusher as shown. Attach the eye bolt in the center of the smaller face. Drill ⅛-inch-diameter-holes on both angled faces.

4.12
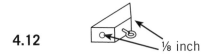
⅛ inch

8. Drill a hole to fit the Wheel Axle in one face of each Footer. Insert the Wheels and Wheel Axle into the hole.

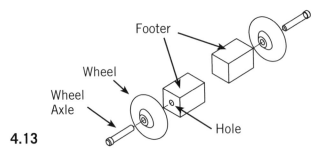

Footer

Wheel

Wheel Axle

4.13

Hole

9. Assemble the Spring Frame by connecting the Spring Frame members together as shown. The best way to construct the frame is to use doweled joints. This means you drill holes in the two pieces to be connected and insert a wooden dowel and glue. This makes for a good, strong joint. If this is not possible, pieces can be nailed together, although the end result will not be as strong.

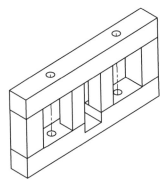

4.14

10. Drill a ½-inch-diameter hole in each Vertical Windlass Support member at a point ⅝ inches from one end. You'll need to measure this carefully.

½-inch holes

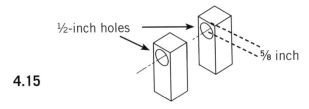

⅝ inch

4.15

11. Next, assemble the Windlass by connecting the Windlass Frame members. Attach the Vertical Windlass Frame members to the Horizontal Windlass Frame member as shown in **diagram 4.16**.

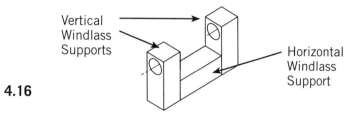

Vertical Windlass Supports

Horizontal Windlass Support

4.16

12. Insert the Windlass Dowel into the Windlass Frame. Then, insert the Windlass Turning Pegs into the ⅛-inch holes in the Windlass Dowel and glue into place as shown in **diagram 4.17**.

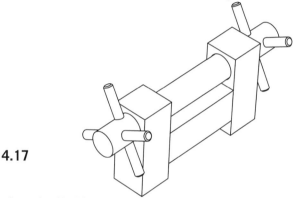

4.17

13. Complete the Ballista by connecting the notched end of the Bed to the Spring Frame, and the other end to the Windlass Frame. If using glue, let dry.

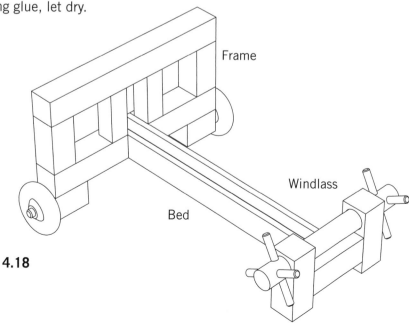

Frame

Windlass

Bed

4.18

14. Wind the Torsion Springs. To do this, loop your cord several times through the holes in the Upper and Lower Spring Frame and then insert the washers and Turning Dowels. (You may experiment with different types of cords to see which works the best. Nylon and polypropylene work well, but natural fiber twines such as cotton, sisal, and jute may be tried as well.) Pull the cord medium tight and then tie off. Place Throwing Arms in each cord and then twist the looped cord outboard (so that the Throwing Arms are pulled towards the outside) until there are many twists in the cord. There should be an equal number of twists above the throwing arm as below. As the cord twists, they will tightly grip the throwing arm (called the braccium by the Greeks) and push it against the head frame. Do this by first twisting the upper dowel and then twisting the bottom dowel, going back and forth between them until they are both tight and there is approximately the same amount of tension on both. When tight, lock the spring into place with the Stop Peg. Repeat the procedure on the other spring.

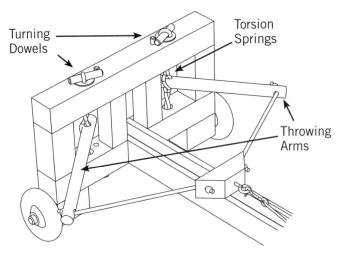

Turning Dowels

Torsion Springs

Throwing Arms

4.19

15. Connect the Pusher to the Throwing Arm by running cords from the ⅛-inch hole on each Throwing Arm to the holes on the Pusher. Tie off securely.

16. Wind the Windlass Cord. Run the Windlass Cord through the loop end of the hook. Then, using a staple or small nail, attach the ends of the cord to the Windlass Dowel at a point about 2½ inches from either end. Attach the hook to the eye bolt.

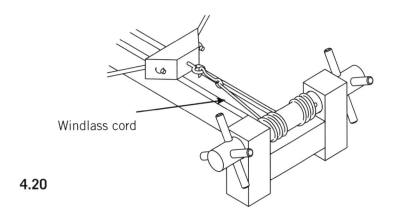

Windlass cord

4.20

17. The Ballista is now ready to fire.
18. To operate your model Ballista, retract the Pusher by using the Windlass Turning Pegs. When the Pusher is retracted, place suitable ammunition—a peanut, or something similar—on the Bed. To fire, release the hook.

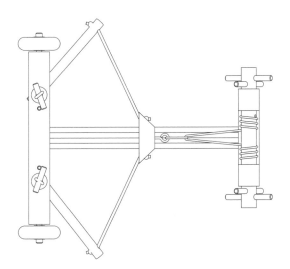

4.21

The Slings of the Ancients

Adult supervision required

👓 Use protective eyewear

⬤ Flying object alert: Use care when aiming and firing

A BALEARIC HAND SLING

Warning! Using a sling can be dangerous! This experiment requires responsible adult supervision. There are some specific rules for making and using a sling.

First of all, it will take a while to learn how to use a sling with skill. Your initial shots will go nowhere near where you are aiming, because aiming and releasing the sling takes a lot of practice to get right. So, only perform the experiment in a suitable place, making certain that there isn't anyone or anything nearby that could be hurt by a misaimed shot.

Second, use only soft, non-damaging ammunition in your sling. Water balloons are often used, but even a water balloon can be dangerous if it hits the wrong thing, such as a person!

You can build a sling, just like a catapult uses, in order to throw things farther than you could without the sling action. "Sling action" is a complex and wonderful thing. Almost every catapult ever built took advantage of the extra distance that sling action adds to the typical throw.

A hand sling allows you to throw stuff farther than you could with just your arm because the sling increases both the length of your arm and the velocity of the object at release. Using a sling is like having a six-foot-long arm, kind of like a gorilla!

The following section shows how to build and use a simple hand sling. But, first, a little history.

> And David put his hand in his bag and took out a stone, and slung it, and struck the Philistine on his forehead; the stone sank into his forehead, and he fell on his face to the ground.
>
> —Book of Samuel

Almost everyone has heard the biblical story of David and Goliath. David, a young Jewish shepherd, fought and killed the nine-foot-tall Philistine using only a small rope sling and five smooth stones he took from a nearby brook.

The sling has been an effective weapon since ancient times. The armies of Alexander the Great used mercenary soldiers from Rhodes, who were eagerly recruited because of their well-known skill and accuracy using a sling. A proficient slinger was every bit as important a soldier as an archer, and in some places even more highly valued. Despite the simplicity of the weapon (after all, it is basically just a length of cord with a pouch in the middle), a skilled slinger could hit a moving target from a hundred yards away or more with deadly force and accuracy.

In Alexander's time, there were a number of tribes and regions known for training good slingers—the Island of Rhodes, the city of Thrace, the country of Persia. But the best slingers were said to be the men and boys from the Balearic Islands. (The Balearic Islands are in the western section of the Mediterranean, off the coast of modern Spain.) It was said by one classical writer, "Balearic mothers compel them while still young boys to use the sling continually. Every day, they set up before them a piece of bread fastened to a stake, and they are not permitted to eat until he has hit the bread."

MATERIALS

- (1) 22-inch length of cotton cord
- (1) 18-inch length of cotton cord
- (1) 16-inch by 6-inch oval cut piece of cotton fabric

DIRECTIONS

1. Securely attach one cord to each end of the sling as shown in the photograph below.

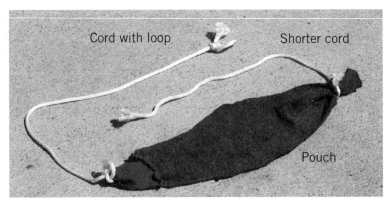

4.22

2. Tie a wrist loop in the 22-inch length of cord.

OPERATING THE HAND SLING

Using a Hand Sling takes lots (and lots!) of practice. At first, it will be hard to even send the missile going in the right direction. But with practice, a person can get good enough to hit a moving target from many feet away. Follow the instructions in **diagram 4.23** to get the basics of hand-slinging.

1. Load the sling with a water balloon or other suitable ammunition.
2. Loop the free end of the longer cord around your wrist, tight enough so it won't fall off when you throw the ammunition. Hold the free end of the other cord between your thumb and forefinger.
3. Hold the Hand Sling overhead and then rotate the sling three or four times. Most of the rotation should be done by your wrist instead of your arm.

4. When the balloon is going fast enough, (three or four rotations is about all that's needed), let the free end of the cord go from between your fingers, at about the point shown in **diagram 4.23**.

4.23

A THRACIAN STAFF SLING

The staff sling is a unique type of sling. It was used in battles by Thracian soldiers called Peltasts, or slingers. The Peltasts were lightly armed, fast-moving foot soldiers who ran in, threw their stone or javelin, and ran away before they could be pursued.

There are advantages and disadvantages to the staff sling. On the plus side, a staff sling is much (much!) easier to aim. But the velocity of the water balloon or other object thrown by a staff sling is considerably less than a projectile thrown with a hand sling.

MATERIALS

- (1) wooden pole approximately 4 feet long, between 1 and 2 inches in diameter
- Hammer
- (1) headless nail
- Balearic Hand Sling

DIRECTIONS

1. Hammer a headless nail into the top end of a stout 4-foot pole. Hammer the nail straight in, but be sure to leave 1 inch of nail exposed.
2. Take the Balearic Hand Sling and remove the wrist loop knot. Replace the wrist loop with a loop about 1 inch in diameter on the 22-inch-long cord.
3. Securely tie the other end to a point about 18 inches below the end of the staff with the nail. Refer to the diagram to see how this looks.

OPERATING THE THRACIAN STAFF SLING

Refer to the drawing here to learn how to use the Thracian Staff Sling. All safety precautions mentioned in the Balearic Hand Sling section apply here as well.

1. Place the small loop you tied in Step 2 over the headless nail.
2. Hold the staff at a comfortable angle and place your ammunition (e.g., a small water balloon) in the sling.
3. Grasp the Staff Sling with both hands and with a smooth overhead motion, lob the ammo at your chosen target.

You can vary the length of the sling and move the tied end up and down on the staff to see what provides the best results.

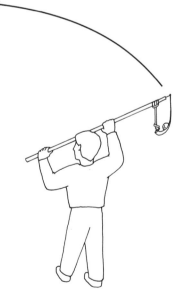

4.24

5

TO THE LAST MAN

JOTAPATA

"Now is the time," roared Joseph ben Matiyahu, the leader of the Jews in first-century Israel, to his followers, "to begin the combat, when all hope of deliverance is past. Fine is it to sacrifice life for renown and by some glorious exploit to ensure memory in posterity!"

Soon after these words were spoken in 67 CE, the legions of Roman emperor Nero began their assault on the hilltop fortress of the Jews, Jotapata. Nero's general in charge, Vespasian, ordered his siege weapons forward. On Vespasian's command, more than 160 onagers and ballista began their assault on the great fortress on the hill.

Despite the constant hail of stones and arrows from the machines, the grimly determined defenders held on. These were the original zealots, the people for whom the term was invented, and unsurprisingly, they were unwilling to surrender, no matter how outmatched they were in men and weapons. One defender, Eleazar ben Sameas, hurled an enormous stone from atop a fortress wall at the Roman battering ram attacking it. The chroniclers of the battle said the stone crashed into the ram, "with such force that he broke off the ram's head; then, leaping down, Eleazar carried off this trophy from the midst of the enemy and bore it with perfect composure to the foot of the ramparts" despite being shot with five Roman arrows. From there, the wounded Eleazar climbed back up "the wall and there stood conspicuous to all the admirers of his bravery; then, writhing under his wounds, he fell headlong with the ram's head in his hands."

But individual acts of bravery notwithstanding, the Roman catapults were numerous and very, very powerful. This eyewitness historical account gives a few examples of this.

> Some incidents of that night will give an idea of the force of the Roman engines. One of the men standing on the wall beside Joseph ben Matiyahu had his head carried away by a stone, and his skull was shot, as from a sling, to a distance of three furlongs. More alarming even than the engines was their whirring drone, more frightful than the missiles the crash.

On the 47th day of the siege, the Romans completed a ramp that allowed the legions to enter the fortress. Despite a desperate battle, the far more numerous Romans quickly defeated the Jews, most of whom were either slain by the Romans or committed suicide.

The Magnet-Powered Onager

Adult supervision required

 Use protective eyewear

 Swinging arm alert: Watch out for moving arms or levers

 Sharp and/or heavy tool advisory: Project requires use of saw or hammer

 Flying object alert: Use care when aiming and firing

5.1 Onager

We've already seen how rope springs are used to provide the energy
needed to hurl projectiles. The Romans improved the Greek catapult
by using a single, very large rope spring and turning it horizontally.
This made it more powerful and more reliable. They called this style
of catapult the onager. There are many ways besides twisted rope
to store and release the energy needed to move the arms of a great
catapult. This project uses an unusual source of power: magnets.

As you may already know, in any magnet, the magnetic forces are
concentrated around the ends. These ends are called poles and there
is a north pole and a south pole. While the two poles may look the
same, they act differently. If you place the south pole of a magnet
near the north pole of another magnet, you will see and feel them
attract one another. But if you place two similar poles, like north to
north or south to south, near one another you will find that they repel
one another. We will use this idea to build a fairly powerful table top
catapult.

While there are no records of any ancient catapult maker actually
using magnets to power their siege weapon, this off-beat project
is both fun and educational, and would make a great science fair
project!

MATERIALS

- (2) 1-inch by 4-inch pieces of wood, 7½ inches long (Sides)
- (1) 1-inch by 4-inch piece of wood, 8 inches long (Base)
- (4) 1½-inch by ¾-inch by ¾-inch pieces of wood (Feet)
- (1) 1½-inch by ¾-inch by 9-inch-long rectangular piece of wood (You can glue together two ¾-inch square wooden dowels, each 9 inches long, to make this piece if desired)
- (10) ¾-inch-diameter by ¼-inch-thick round magnets. Neodymium magnets are stronger than ceramic magnets and therefore allow the catapult to hurl farther. (Note: strong magnets are a pinching hazard. Handle very carefully! Young children should not be allowed to handle magnets.)
- (1) 1-inch-wide utility hinge and screws
- (1) 1½-inch-long finish nail
- Saw
- Hammer
- Screwdriver
- Electric drill with ¾-inch spade bit
- All-purpose epoxy glue

DIRECTIONS

1. Cut one edge of each Side piece as shown in **diagram 5.2**.

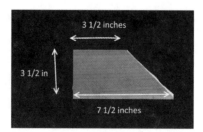

5.2 Sides

2. Use the drill and ¾-inch spade bit to drill five ¼-inch-deep holes in the 1½-inch by ¾-inch by 9-inch-piece of wood following the pattern described in **diagram 5.3**.

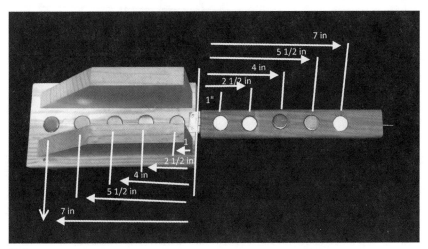

5.3

3. Use the drill and ¾-inch spade bit to drill five ¼-inch deep holes in the center of the 8-inch-long 1-inch by 4-inch Base following the pattern described in the same diagram.

    Important: the holes on both pieces of wood must align exactly.

4. Note which side of each magnet is north and which is south. To do this, dot the face of one magnet with a red marker. Then use that magnet to find the repelling face and mark that face with a red dot as well. Glue the magnets into the holes with the red dots facing out.

5. Attach the ¾-inch by 1½-inch throwing arm to the 1-inch by 4-inch by 8-inch base piece with the hinge as shown in **diagram 5.4**. Test for correct magnet polarity by pressing down on the throwing arm and making sure it springs back up.

5.4

6. Attach the two side pieces to the base as shown in **diagram 5.5** using epoxy.

5.5

7. Glue the feet to the base.

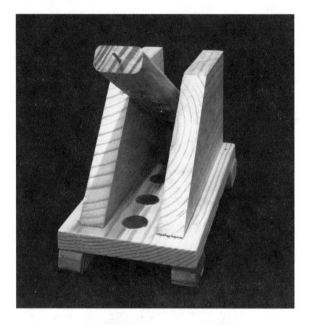

5.6

8. Use the hammer to pound in the finish nail in the center of the end of the moving arm as shown **diagram 5.6**.

Your magnetic tabletop catapult is complete. Tie one end of a short piece string to an object that you want to use as a projectile and the other end into a loop.

Place the loop over the finish nail and then press down on the throwing arm. When you release, the magnetic force will hurl the object!

6

A BLACK FLAG FLIES OVER ACRE

SALADIN, RICHARD, AND THE THIRD CRUSADE

s rough, dangerous, and bloody as a medieval siege was, there were still "rules of engagement" that both sides generally followed. The rules allowed both sides to communicate, at least a little bit, since there were no radios or telephones, and most people couldn't read. When the leader of one side wanted to deliver a message to the leader of the other, they would often send a herald, or messenger, to deliver the message. More often than not the other side allowed the messenger to come and go safely, but on occasion bad things could happen to the messenger. For instance, during the Hundred Years War between the French and English, a herald carrying a message from the English was taken prisoner. Evidently, the French were in a particularly bad mood that day, for the poor man was shot back into the English encampment at Auberoche, from a catapult, with the message tied around his neck. It was later written that the knights there "were much astonished and discomfited when they saw him arrive."

With such danger present, it no doubt became difficult to convince someone to visit the other side with a message, especially if the siege had been particularly long or cruel. Therefore, a system of signals or customs evolved between warring armies that allowed them a very basic way to communicate from afar. For instance, if an army showed up at a fortress or castle, they could signify their intent to besiege the castle by throwing a spear at the front gate. After the siege had begun, if one side wanted to negotiate, it might beat large drums. If the invite was accepted, a messenger would then appear.

The rules of warfare in the time of the Crusades were fluid and changed often. In some cases, if the terms of surrender offered by the besieging army were accepted, the soldiers in the castle would raise a white flag. And, if the soldiers inside would not give up, if they planned to fight to the last man, then high above the castle they'd hoist the black flag. The black flag was a very intimidating and frightening sign, for no quarter, or mercy, was to be given and none expected!

Starting in the year 1096, armies of European soldiers traveled eastward from England, France, Germany, and elsewhere to win control of the Middle East from the Muslims. For the next two hundred years, successive waves of armies traveled by horseback, foot, and ship to fight the Muslim armies and take control of the places important to their Christian faith, most important of which was the city of Jerusalem. Territories were won and lost, first Muslim, then Christian, then Muslim, back and forth for hundreds of years and through much fighting and loss of life.

In most cases, the type of fighting involved siege warfare, not pitched battles between armies in open fields. As soon as one side took control of a town, they'd build a fort or castle to keep it.

Soon, the other side would lay siege, building catapults of all sorts, and try to win it back, this going on in fits and spurts. Some say that it continues on, in a fashion, through the present day.

One of the most famous battles of the Crusades took place at a town called Acre in the years around 1190. Acre is on the coast of modern-day Israel, and in 1190 it was a very important location, commanding the seacoast as well as land routes north and south through the entire area.

Many of Europe's most famous rulers brought their armies eastward to fight in the Third Crusade. From Germany came the warrior-emperor Frederick Barbarossa; from France came King Philip Augustus, and from England came the best and most famous warrior of them all, Richard Coeur de Lion, known as Richard the Lionheart.

Philip Augustus arrived first and ordered the construction of a few siege engines, but nothing much came of it. In June Richard arrived, and from that moment he took command of the siege. Although technically European kings only commanded their own troops, it was Richard who was clearly in control of the entire operation. Although a man of middling intellect, he was the type of energetic and charismatic leader that the crusading armies needed. He rallied all of the men, and made them eager and anxious to fight the Muslims, whom they called "Saracens." But the Muslim armies had a leader that was more than a match for him—their own famous king, Saladin. Salah al-Din Yusuf bin Ayub, or Saladin as he is popularly known, was the ruler of Egypt and known in Arab histories as "the Great Sultan." Saladin is one of the very few historical figures of the Crusades who was thought highly of by historians from both sides of the conflict. His name translates to "righteousness of the faith," and by many, but not all, accounts he was a most noble and valiant leader.

During the Third Crusade, the Franks (as all the French soldiers and their allies were called) made a great effort to take Acre, launching an intense siege of the city. But whenever the Frankish armies pressed the city too closely, Saladin would call up troops from all over his kingdom and send them in to attack the Christian camps. Saladin did not have an army strong enough to wage an all-out, pitched battle against so large an army as Richard commanded, but he was strong enough to divide their attention and keep them from overrunning Acre, at least for a while.

Despite these sporadic attacks from the Muslim troops, the Franks continued the siege in earnest. Richard and Philip set their soldiers to work building defenses from the enemies' slings and arrows, high siege towers, and catapults of many sorts to attack Acre's walls. They erected dozens, even scores of catapults, mostly traction-operated, but it is likely they built and used all types of catapults—torsion-powered onagers to attack men on the ramparts, tension-powered spring engines capable of hurling a barrage of iron arrows in a pitched ground battle, and the big, rock-hurling, gravity-powered trebuchets to knock down stone walls. One of the most successful catapults at Acre was named God's Stone Thrower, a big and powerful traction catapult. Building it was a major project that occupied many soldiers, both French and English.

In addition to the artillery, the Franks built huge, movable siege towers with which to attack Acre's thick protective walls. Under the covering fire provided by the rock- and arrow-throwing machines, they built several movable towers, the biggest of which were called Mal Voisin, which means "bad neighbor," and Mal Cousine, which means "bad relation." These towers were said to be 60 cubits (90 feet) tall and covered with animal skins that were treated with vinegar, mud, and fire-resistant substances. These towers could be filled with armed men and then moved against the city's walls. Once in place, the fighting men could jump or run from the siege tower over a swinging bridge and beyond the city walls to the inside of the city.

The Muslims inside Acre's protective walls watched the Europeans build the huge siege towers and were worried. Such large towers were indeed a big threat. But what could they do? They watched as the Franks began to fill up the moat surrounding Acre with dirt. Under the cover of archers and massed catapults, including God's Stone Thrower, the Franks could wheel the large towers into place. Once next to the fortress walls, the hordes of Crusader fighting men could easily climb or leap down from the siege towers into the city. The Muslims inside Acre were convinced they were doomed—that is, until a soldier from Damascus spoke up.

"Let us build a catapult," he said, "one that shoots unquenchable fire that will burn up even those well-protected siege towers. I know how to make such a substance."

His friends looked at him with amazement. It turned out that this man had long experimented with shooting fire from catapults. The worried commander of Acre had no better idea and told the soldier to go ahead. So he mixed up large batches of a special chemical compound and poured it into barrels.

As this was occurring, the Christian siege towers were coming closer every minute. Soon they would be in position to make the attack. With little time to spare, the Muslims shot at the besiegers' towers several barrels of a different fiery substance, one that did not start the specially protected towers burning. The Franks laughed when they saw this and taunted the Muslim soldiers from their siege towers.

"Ha!" laughed the Frankish soldiers. "Your catapults are no match for our indestructible siege towers! Prepare to be invaded!" But these first projectiles were just a ruse, thrown to allow the catapult crew to find the right range and direction to hit the oncoming siege towers squarely, without inducing the Crusaders to actually leave the siege towers. Once the firing crews had the siege towers dead in their sights, barrel after barrel of the new and terrible incendiary mixture fell upon the siege towers, shot from inside Acre's walls by a group of gravity-powered trebuchets and traction-style catapults. Despite their protection, the wooden towers of Mal Voisin and Mal Cousine quickly caught fire and burned down in a roaring inferno of smoke and flame. Hundreds of Crusaders were killed and hurt. The Muslims rejoiced and the Christians howled and wept with anger. Bolstered by the victory, the Muslims decided to fight on with new conviction and ferocity. From atop the battlements of the city's protective walls, the black flag was raised. No surrender!

The siege of Acre continued with much bloodshed and much destruction. It went on for days, for weeks, for months. Both sides built large and powerful catapults. Attacks and counterattacks were made. Raids were carried out with both sides first gaining and then losing the advantage. In a last great effort, the Christian army mined the walls protecting Acre—that is, they dug tunnels underneath them—and then threw stone after stone against them from a host of torsion- and gravity-powered catapults. Finally, in July of 1191, Richard and his armies broke through Acre's walls and the Crusader army flooded in through the breach. Richard took control of the city. It was time, finally, for the weary Muslims to surrender.

The black flag came down. The white flag was raised over Acre.

Of the three European kings who started out on this crusade, Richard was now in sole command. Philip Augustus fell ill and returned to France, and Frederick Barbarossa had drowned crossing a river. One of Richard's first acts after taking control of Acre was to do something that has earned him condemnation from modern historians. He was holding a large number of Muslim prisoners as hostages and Richard ordered the execution of them all, declaring that Saladin had broken the terms of the surrender agreement. Two thousand seven hundred prisoners were killed—men, women, and children. They were executed outside the city walls; Saladin's soldiers could see the massacre, which took all day, and tried to rescue them. Even as the prisoners were being slaughtered, a battle was fought, but the Muslims were driven back and all the prisoners died. A sad and terrible day!

God's Stone Thrower: A Traction-Style Catapult

Adult supervision required

 Use protective eyewear

 Swinging arm alert: Watch out for moving arms or levers

 Sharp and/or heavy tool advisory: Project requires use of saw or hammer

 Flying object alert: Use care when aiming and firing

A traction catapult is powered by human muscles. Typically, it consists of a pole or lever arm that pivots. A person pulls down as hard as possible on the shorter end, which makes the longer end spin very fast. The fast-moving end is capable of shooting a projectile much farther and higher than a person could ever simply throw it.

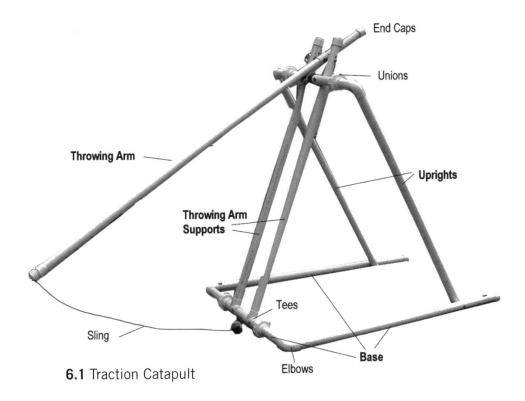

6.1 Traction Catapult

WORKING WITH PVC OR PLASTIC PIPE

You'll have to learn how to work with PVC pipe to make God's Stone Thrower. This section will explain how to make safe and secure PVC joints.

First, you should be aware that there are at least four types of plastic pipe and plastic pipe joints available: PVC, CPVC, ABS, and PB. The letters are abbreviations of the type of plastic material that composes the pipe. Pressure-rated, schedule 40 PVC pipe and pipe fittings are made of white polyvinyl chloride. This is the type of pipe and pipe fittings recommended for making this catapult, but ABS is an acceptable substitute.

Both PVC and ABS are pretty tough materials, but they will break or crack if mistreated. When operating the catapult, be sure not to place more stress on the frame or throwing arm than the assembly can handle. If it starts to flex too much, crack, or come apart, stop immediately and make repairs. Also, PVC is weaker in very warm or cold weather, so take note of that fact.

PVC pipe is easily cut with a regular hand saw. It is important that all the cuts be made as close to 90 degrees to the centerline of the pipe as possible. That way, you won't leave any interior gaps, which will weaken the joint.

The directions tell you to "dry fit" the pipe into the fittings before you apply any cement. This is important because it allows you to see how well you've measured and cut while there is still time to make changes. Sometimes the dry-fitted pipes and joint fittings stick together so tightly it is hard to get them apart. If that happens, carefully whack the fitting loose with a wooden block.

Joining and gluing, or cementing, PVC pipe is technically called "solvent welding." The solvent melts the PVC contact surfaces before you push the pipe and the pipe fitting together, then the two parts fuse together as the solvent evaporates. Each type of plastic pipe has its own special solvent. Some solvents are advertised to work on several types of plastic, but it is strongly recommended that you use the solvent that is meant solely for the type of plastic you're working with.

The solvent works only on CLEAN surfaces—no dirt, no grease, and no moisture. Wipe the inside of the fitting and the outside of the pipe with a clean cloth. Then apply PVC primer (called "purple primer") to the ends.

Next, coat the surfaces that you want to join with a liberal amount of PVC solvent. This PVC solvent should only be used in well-ventilated areas. Push the pipe into the pipe fitting quickly and give it a one-quarter turn as you seat it. Hold it tight for about 15 seconds, and voilà—you're done!

Be sure to observe the cure times shown on the PVC cement bottle's directions. The solvent is flammable, so keep open flames away from solvent and solvent fumes.

MATERIALS

- Hand saw
- Masking tape
- PVC primer ("purple primer")
- Drill and drill bits
- Sandpaper
- Rubber mallet
- PVC solvent

The Base

- (2) 5-foot pieces of 1½-inch-diameter PVC pipe
- (2) 8½-inch pieces of 1½-inch-diameter PVC pipe
- (2) 3-inch pieces of 1½-inch-diameter PVC pipe
- (1) 6-inch piece of 1½-inch-diameter PVC pipe (cut piece after dry fitting procedure, see page 80)
- (2) 1½-inch-diameter PVC pipe unions. (A "union" is a specific fitting that allows you to connect two non-rotating pipes together. Ask for these at larger hardware and home stores. If you cannot find one locally, they may be ordered on the Internet; search under "1½ in. PVC Slip x Slip Union.")
- (2) 1½-inch-diameter 90-degree PVC elbow fittings
- (2) 1½-inch-diameter PVC tee fittings
- (2) ¼-inch-diameter bolt, 5 inches long, with washers and nut
- (2) 1½-inch-diameter PVC end caps

The Uprights

- (2) 5-foot pieces of 1½-inch-diameter PVC pipe
- (2) 5-inch pieces of 1½-inch-diameter PVC pipe
- (1) 18-inch piece of 1½-inch-diameter PVC pipe (cut piece after dry fitting procedure, see directions)
- (2) 1½-inch-diameter 90-degree PVC elbow fittings
- (2) 1½-inch-diameter PVC pipe unions

The Throwing Arm Supports

- (2) 5-foot pieces of 1½-inch-diameter PVC pipe
- (2) 1½-inch-diameter PVC end caps
- (1) 10-inch, ½-inch-diameter bolt or eye bolt with nut and washer
- (2) ½-inch-diameter bolts, 5 inches long, with washers and nut

The Throwing Arm

- (1) 85-inch piece of 1½-inch-diameter PVC pipe
- (1) threaded adapter with ¼-inch hole
- (1) threaded PVC end cap
- (1) ¼-inch-diameter bolt, 1½ inches long
- (1) 1½-inch-diameter coupling, both sides smooth

Ammunition

- (1) Tennis ball, mounted on 3- to 4-foot rope sling with loop in end (Note: you may use other ammunition as well, including water balloons, with a 3- to 4-foot string tied to the end. However, be certain that any ammunition shot will not hurt people or property.)

DIRECTIONS

1. Using a saw, carefully cut all PVC pieces to the lengths specified in the materials list, except for the 6-inch PVC pipe in the Base and the 18-inch PVC pipe in the Upright. Because PVC plumbing fittings are often made by different manufacturers, these pieces may vary slightly in their dimensions. Cut these last, at Step 8 below, and be prepared to make them a little longer or shorter in order to get a good overall fit. Label each piece with masking tape to keep them from being mixed up.
2. Remove any excess plastic or "burrs" left on the cut end so they are nice and smooth. You can use a file or sandpaper if necessary.
3. Lay out all the materials and the directions in front of you. Make sure you have enough room to lay out and glue your parts.

4. Drill holes and then dry fit the parts for the Base, as shown in **diagram 6.2**. DO NOT cement the pieces at this point.

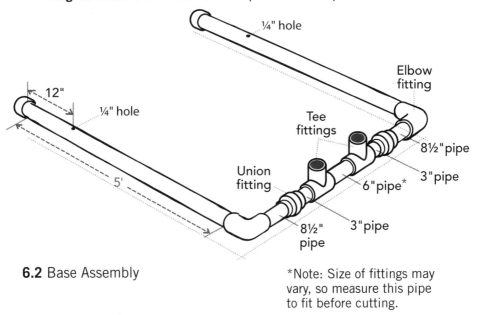

¼" hole

Elbow fitting

12"

¼" hole

Tee fittings

8½" pipe

3" pipe

Union fitting

6" pipe*

5'

8½" pipe

3" pipe

6.2 Base Assembly

*Note: Size of fittings may vary, so measure this pipe to fit before cutting.

5. Dry fit the parts for the Uprights, as shown.

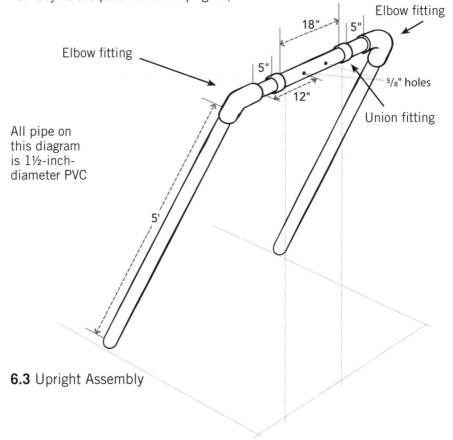

Elbow fitting

18"

5"

Elbow fitting

5"

5/8" holes

12"

Union fitting

All pipe on this diagram is 1½-inch-diameter PVC

5'

6.3 Upright Assembly

6. Dry fit the Throwing Arm Supports together.

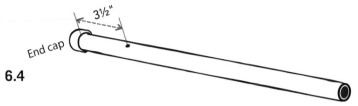

6.4

7. Drill a hole for the ¼-inch bolt in the Throwing Arm end cap and then screw it into place using a nut. The bolt will protrude out from the end of the Throwing Arm as shown in **diagram 6.6**.

8. Assemble the catapult by attaching the dry fitted Base, Uprights, and Throwing Arm Supports together. Cut the 6-inch PVC pipe in the Base and the 18-inch PVC pipe in the Upright last in order to get a good overall fit.

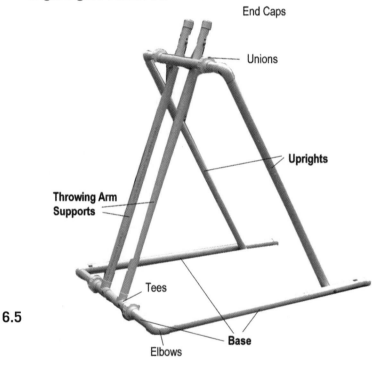

6.5

9. Using a portable drill, drill clearance holes in the 5-foot Throwing Arm Support PVC pipes as shown in **diagram 6.4**. Use a helper to hold the assembly in place while drilling the holes. (Note: the holes for the bolts that connect the Throwing Arm Supports to the Upright are drilled at an angle. Have your helper hold the assembling firmly in place while you drill.)

10. Make a piece to reinforce the Throwing Arm where it pivots. Take the 1½-inch smooth coupling and sand the interior to remove any ridges. Continue to sand or file down the interior surface until you can just slide the tube over the Throwing Arm to a point 12 inches from one end. The sliding fit should be tight, so you may need to knock the reinforcing tube into place with a hammer and wooden block. You may solvent weld into place if necessary. The drawing below shows where the reinforcing piece is to be placed.

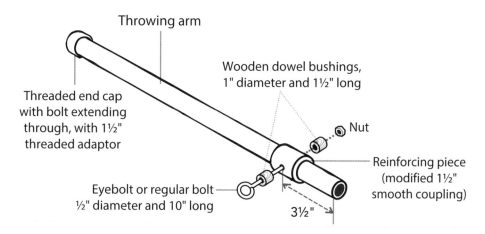

Throwing arm

Wooden dowel bushings,
1" diameter and 1½" long

Threaded end cap
with bolt extending
through, with 1½"
threaded adaptor

Nut

Reinforcing piece
(modified 1½"
smooth coupling)

Eyebolt or regular bolt
½" diameter and 10" long

3½"

6.6

11. Drill a ½-inch hole in the Throwing Arm through the reinforced section, as shown above. Then, insert the ½-inch-diameter 10-inch bolt through the Throwing Arm and Throwing Arm supports. (Note: You may find it helpful to insert cylindrical wooden bushings on the 10-inch bolt to keep the Throwing Arm centered on the catapult. Place these on either side of the Throwing Arm. To make the two wooden bushings, simply drill a ½-inch hole in the middle of a 1-inch-diameter dowel. The bushings should be 1½ inches long.)

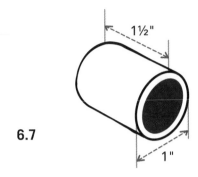

6.7

12. Dry fit everything together by carefully engaging all pipes into their fittings. Use light force from a rubber mallet if necessary. All parts should be aligned and the entire assembly neat and square. The photo at the beginning of this project shows how the catapult is supposed to look. Does it look good? If it does, you're ready to cement it all into place. If not, re-cut the pipes where necessary to get everything squared up.

13. Carefully disassemble the catapult and reassemble, piece by piece, using cement to permanently place each piece according the diagrams. Important: Do not cement union fittings! (Hint: Make the letters A, B, C, and D in indelible marker on the male and female ends of each pair of mated union pieces so you can quickly tell which unions go together when setting up the catapult.) Use extra care when cementing the tee fittings on the Base, so that they maintain the correct angle to the ground.

Your human-powered traction catapult is now ready!

OPERATING THE CATAPULT

1. The catapult has been designed with union fittings to allow you to break down the catapult for easy transport. The fittings simply screw into place and unscrew. To assemble the catapult, attach the male to female end of the unions.

2. The ammunition for God's Stone Thrower is attached to a short rope sling that is part of the ammunition itself. Because the sling gets tossed along with the ammo, it is referred to as a "sacrificial sling." If you use a tennis ball or potato as

ammunition, attach a 2-foot cord to the tennis ball or spud, and then tie a 1-inch-diameter loop in the free end. Similarly, if you shoot water balloons, you will need to tie a 2-foot string around the knotted end of the balloon. Then, tie a 1-inch-diameter loop in the other end of the string. Place the loop end around the ¼-inch bolt sticking out from the end of the Throwing Arm.

3. Firmly grasp the short end of the Throwing Arm and pull smartly toward the ground. The long end will swing up and over before being stopped by the cross arm of the uprights. The tennis ball sling will fly up and away, sailing towards the target in a high, looping arc.

4. You can change the maximum height and distance by experimenting with the length of the sling. You will find that a very short sling launches the ball very high and short. A longer sling provides less height and more distance.

KEEPING SAFETY IN MIND

1. Watch your hands and fingers! If you put them in the wrong place, they could get pinched.

2. The areas in back of and in front of the traction catapult are danger zones. If the sling leaves the arm too early, the projectile could go straight up, or even backward! Keep everyone away from the Throwing Arm and make sure that there is no one in front of or in back of the catapult who could get hit with the projectile or by the moving arm.

3. Inspect the joints often to make sure they are tight and there are no cracks or other problems. Replace worn pieces promptly.

4. Check local laws to see if there are any ordinances regulating such devices.

Detail of throwing arm's end

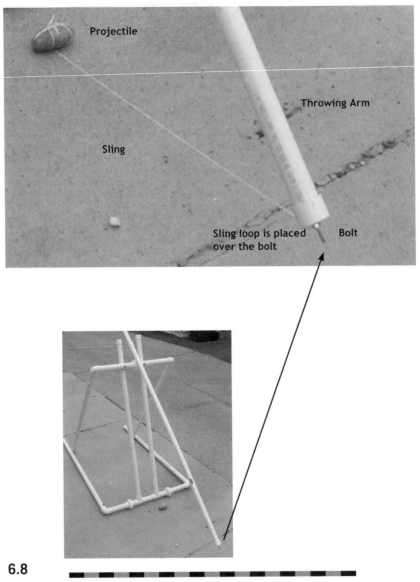

6.8

THE GREAT KHAN'S CATAPULTS

As many stories in this book attest, a siege is a difficult undertaking. One of the longest sieges in history occurred in 13th-century China, when Kublai Kahn and his Mongol army besieged the Chinese city of Xiangyang from 1268 until early 1273. Kublai was the grandson of Genghis Khan and one of the most powerful kings in history. At the peak of his power the size of his realm rivaled that of Alexander the Great.

After taking control of the northern portions of what is today northern China, Kublai proclaimed himself Emperor of all China, which meant he'd have to conquer the southern part the country as well. Quite naturally, the then-existing Chinese Song dynasty emperor, Duzong, did not think highly of this idea and arrayed his substantial military forces for battle.

THE SEIGE OF XIANGYANG

The two armies came together at Xiangyang, a city in central China about 500 miles west of modern-day Shanghai. Emperor Duzong appointed his general Lu Wen-huan to defend the city.

The commanders took stock of their situation. Xiangyang was a powerful city, with enough food to last years. Importantly, the Song soldiers they commanded were well trained and well armed, and the city's defenses included large, powerful catapults, capable of hitting targets far away.

In 1268 the fast-riding Mongols surrounded Xiangyang and blockaded the river in and out of the city. The long siege had begun.

The siege lasted for several years and throughout that time, Emperor Duzong remained defiant—he would not submit to Kublai and his Mongols. There were many attempts made by the Song to escape the siege, but each time they tried to escape, the Mongols forced them back inside.

Eventually, Kublai Khan reached his limit. Something had to be done to break the stalemate. He sent a message to his nephew, Abakha, the ruler of Persia. Abakha ordered two renowned engineers, Isma'il of Hilla and Ala al-Din of Mosul, to travel to the siege and there construct a number of large trebuchets. The trebuchets the Persians built were enormous beasts of machines, and they were given the name hui-hui pao, which means "Muslim trebuchets."

The chroniclers of the battle wrote that the gigantic trebuchets shook heaven and earth when they fired and the projectiles destroyed everything they hit. Since they were so large, they could throw much farther than the trebuchets that the Song Chinese had to defend themselves. Therefore, they could be placed far away, outside the range of the defenders' machines, and still bombard the city with accuracy.

The boulders that the Mongol machines threw weighed hundreds of pounds. After some time, the trebuchets were outfitted with a new type of ammunition with the wonderfully descriptive name of "thunder crash bomb." The bomb was an early type of grenade made out of a hollow iron ball filled with gunpowder. In fact, this was one of the earliest battles in which gunpowder played a role.

The rain of explosives and boulders upon the city was unrelenting. Seeing no way to hold out, Lu Wen-huan surrendered, and the long, long siege finally ended. Soon after, the Mongols conquered the rest of China and Kublai Khan was the sole emperor. The Muslim catapults had done their job.

--- --- --- --- ---

The World's Best Tabletop Catapult

Adult supervision required

 Use protective eyewear

 Swinging arm alert: Watch out for moving arms or levers

 Sharp and/or heavy tool advisory: Project requires use of saw or hammer

 Flying object alert: Use care when aiming and firing

When Isma'il of Hilla and Ala al-Din of Mosul built a hurling machine, they went all out and built the very best. Similarly, the design that follows combines the power of six independent springs allowing you to construct a tabletop catapult model that combines great power with great accuracy. Whether you throw marshmallows or your own version of "thunder crash" malted milk balls with it, you'll find it to be an excellent performer.

MATERIALS

- (1) 1-inch by 6-inch pine board, 11 inches long
- (1) 1-inch by 6-inch pine board, 4 inches long
- (2) 2-inch by 4-inch boards, 4 inches long
- (6) 3½-inch-long spring clothespins

- (2) ½-inch square or semi-round dowels, 3 inches long
- (1) ½-inch square dowel, 9 inches long
- (2) ³⁄₁₆-inch round dowels, 3 inches long
- (1) Ping-Pong ball
- Saw
- Knife
- Hot glue gun

HOW TO BUILD THE WORLD'S BEST TABLETOP CATAPULT

1. Cut a 45-degree angle into the two 4-inch long 2x4s. Refer to **diagram 7.1**.

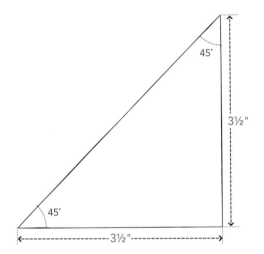

7.1

2. Have an adult cut the Ping-Pong ball in half with the knife. Apply hot glue to the inside of one of the hemispheres and then press the other hemisphere into it. This forms the projectile holding cup.
3. Refer to **diagram 7.2**. Glue the 2x4 pieces you cut in Step 1 onto the 1-inch by 11-inch board as shown.
4. Glue the 1-inch by 4-inch pine board to the angled face of the 2x4s as shown **diagram 7.2**.

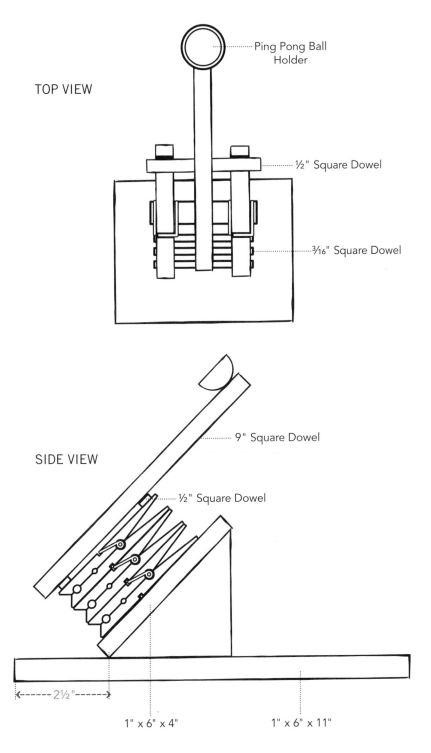

TOP VIEW

Ping Pong Ball
Holder

½" Square Dowel

¾₆" Square Dowel

SIDE VIEW

9" Square Dowel

½" Square Dowel

2½"

1" x 6" x 4"

1" x 6" x 11"

7.2 Assembly diagram

5. Glue the six clothespins to the 1-inch by 4-inch pine board as shown in **diagram 7.3**. Apply glue to the upper and lower sides of the clothespins and let dry.

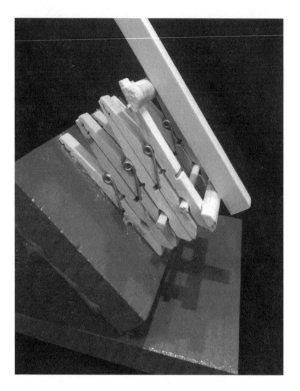

7.3

6. Glue the ³⁄₁₆-inch dowels to the jaws of the clothespins as shown in **diagram 7.3**. These dowels provide lateral stabilization.
7. Glue the 3-inch-long ½-inch-diameter square or semi-round dowels to the top face of the upper clothespin.
8. Glue the 9-inch-long square dowel to the 3-inch-long square dowels.
9. Complete the throwing arm by gluing the throwing cup you made in Step 2 to the top of the 9-inch-long square dowel.
10. Let the glue dry completely before trying out your catapult.

7.4

TO OPERATE THE CATAPULT

This machine is pure simplicity, but that's one reason it works so dependably. Place a piece of ammunition like a marshmallow or a small rubber ball inside the throwing cup. Pull back on the throwing arm. As you do so, you will tense the springs in the clothespins. When you release the throwing arm, the machine will shoot whatever is in the cup across the room.

KEEPING SAFETY IN MIND

1. Don't accidentally place your fingers between the clothespins when pulling back on the arm or they will get pinched!
2. Wear safety glasses when hurling stuff.
3. Don't hurl hard or pointed objects. Don't hurl objects at people who don't want objects hurled at them.

CABULUS, THE GREAT HORSE TREBUCHET

By most accounts, King Philip Augustus of France, whom we first met at the Siege of Acre, was an unusually dour king. He was severe, stern, rather unfriendly, and he was certainly not known for any particularly sharp wit or sense of humor.

Philip Augustus was king of France during a roughly 40-year reign centered around the year 1200 CE. Perhaps his ill temper was due to the fact that his fame and reputation never quite matched that of his English rival, Richard I. In terms of reputation and world opinion, Richard outshone the Frenchman. Even their nicknames show the difference—while Richard was known as Richard Coeur de Lion (Richard the Lionheart), Philip's appellation was merely Philip Augustus. Philip Augustus was certainly a fine name, but not nearly as evocative as his rival's.

But in terms of results of lasting effect, Philip Augustus was head and shoulders above contemporary kings, especially the wonderfully named but slow-witted Richard. At the time of Philip Augustus's ascension to power in 1180, the English kings held far more territory in what is now France than the French royal family did. A map of land holdings for the year 1175 shows English control of French land from Normandy in the north, down through Anjou, west through Brittany, south through the large and powerful land of Acquitaine, and into the southern reaches of modern-day France, to a land called Gascony. Philip Augustus's father, Louis VII, held only the "demesne" ("royal territory") of Paris.

But by the time Philip died in 1223, the situation had changed immensely. The English were driven out of Normandy, Anjou, Brittany, and most of Acquitaine. These lands were now in control of the French royal family. And who was most responsible for removing the English from all these lands? The dour, unheralded, overlooked-by-history Philip Augustus. The English were pushed out of France mostly because Philip Augustus was a better king than Richard the Lionheart. An able military strategist, he managed to do what his predecessors could not—consolidate most of France into one royal domain. Through military action and diplomacy, he seized the territories of Maine, Touraine, Anjou, Brittany, and Normandy from the English crown.

It was unfortunate for the English that their king loved to fight and hated to govern. He chose to spend almost all of his time outside of England, making war on whomever he could find, often without any particularly good reason. His heroic exploits in the Crusades make good reading, but while he was off fighting the Muslims, the power the English had held in France had become very shaky.

While Richard roamed Europe and the Levant in search of a good fight, back in London his advisors were alarmed. "Richard," said the correspondence from his cadre of dukes and earls, "Stop running around Europe and Asia. Come back and attend to matters here at home! Your kingdom in France is at risk!" It took some convincing, but finally Richard did understand that his country's interests in Brittany, Anjou, Gascony, and the rest of France were in danger, and he took some big steps to shore things up. Perhaps the most important thing he did in this regard was to build castles in France to defend his land holdings.

As we discussed earlier, castle building was a tried-and-true way to protect your interests and make it very hard for another ruler to come in and attempt to take over land. Richard, thick-skulled as he was, understood this very well, and therefore designed one of the most impregnable castles ever built. It was located on the River Seine near the key town of Rouen, situated such that any invasion of the English territories in France by Philip Augustus would need to go right past this castle. The castle was built high on a solid rock bluff in such a way that there were cliff-like natural rock faces on three sides of the castle, and on the fourth, the river. This imposing, unassaultable castle was called Chateau Gaillard.

Chateau Gaillard was huge. It was built with three separate rings of tall walls surrounding the inner ward, or "keep." The outer walls were built with large rock towers 30 feet high and walls 11 feet thick! If the English defenders, high on the ramparts, dropped stones, the walls below were set at angles such that the stones would roll and ricochet wildly, making an assault even more dangerous than normal. Indeed, Chateau Gaillard was a very solid and powerful castle, and one that Richard felt sure would save his empire in France.

In 1199 Richard heard that one of the subjects of the Viscount of Limoges had discovered a hidden treasure of Roman gold. The valuable treasure was found in the Duchy of Acquitaine, one of Richard's holdings. No rule of "finders-keepers" applied then, so Richard claimed the gold as his own.

Not so fast, said the Viscount, and yet again Richard was involved in the siege of a French castle, this time called Castle Chaluz, that took him away from England. In terms of tactics or intensity, the Battle of Chaluz wasn't particularly memorable. In fact, the siege was so ordinary that Richard became bored. So, to amuse himself, he took to riding around the castle on horseback, deliberately offering himself as a target to the archers inside. Richard had a fine time dodging arrows and exchanging insults with the besieged Frenchmen. But things didn't work out too well.

One of the defenders, a man named Bertrand de Gourdon, was evidently a very good marksman. Upon seeing the helmetless Richard riding around the castle yet again, yelling insults, he took careful aim with his bow and arrow and shot Richard in the neck.

Richard had been injured before, and this particular wound wasn't nearly as bad as some previous ones he had survived. But medieval battle conditions were quite dirty, and the doctors of the time were more harmful than helpful, so the wound became infected. Richard hung on for a while, but gangrene set in and he died from the wound on April 6, 1199.

Richard had no heirs, so with his death, the throne of England passed to his brother, John. King John, while not nearly the fighter that Richard was, was perhaps a little more practical, and over time he moved to shore up the English holdings in France.

Regardless of whether John or Richard was king of England, Philip Augustus wanted the English out of his backyard. France is ours, he said, and set out to drive the English out of the territories they ruled on Philip's side of the English Channel. Wars and skirmishes between Philip Augustus and John erupted and then faded, this going on in an up and down pattern of activity for years. Things came to a climax in the year 1203, when Philip decided that Chateau Gaillard would be taken by whatever means necessary.

King John's commander of castle, or castellan, was a trusted man named Roger de Lacy. De Lacy, a determined sort of man, resolved to hold the castle no matter what the cost.

Philip was equally determined to take the castle. He decided to spare no expense and brought forth a large and well-supplied army. He instructed his royal engineers and carpenters to begin work on siege engines, big mangonels, smaller onagers, and one very, very large trebuchet. It was called Cabulus, the Great Horse Catapult. It is assumed that Philip was fond of horses, and he likely wanted a machine as powerful as a team of the strongest war horses.

Cabulus was immense, several stories high, with a swing arm and counterweight powerful enough to cast half-ton stones. The stones were specially mined from nearby quarries, as they needed rock that was hard, and heavy, and tough. Philip's master of engines started working immediately on a model for the giant siege engine. (In those days, engineers did not draw up plans for machines on paper. Instead, they built scale models and then built the real thing based on the model.) The master ordered his men to the nearby forest to cut timbers and hew them into shape. Work had begun on Cabulus—Philip's monster wall breaker, the great stone flinger, the Great Horse Catapult.

In February of 1203, after a preliminary siege of about six months, Philip Augustus decided the time for the frontal attack was right. During that six-month span, the French army had busied themselves with all sorts of war preparations. They built wooden walls around their own camp, and a covered walkway for protection against English arrows. They flattened entire hilltops to make suitable platforms for the catapults, so they could be accurately aimed and fired.

Cabulus and the other siege engines flung stone after stone at Chateau Gaillard's towers and outer wall. The towers stood firm, but the wall did not. The French army had sent in miners under the protective cover of the catapults to dig underneath the foundation of the wall. With pick and shovel, the miners worked to remove earth from under the wall. Eventually, enough dirt was taken out so that when the flying stones hit the wall, it gave way. The French overran the outer courtyard, or "ward," and quickly took control of it.

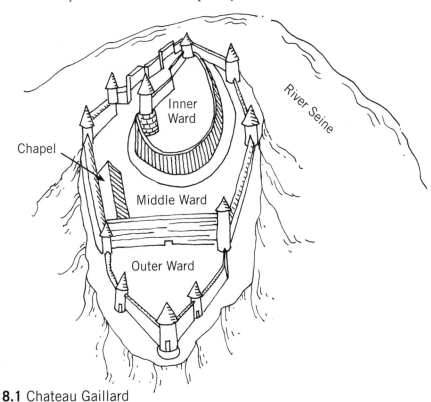

8.1 Chateau Gaillard

101

But the outer ward was just part of the defenses of Chateau Gail-lard. The next task facing the attackers was to take the middle ward, and this was a very hard job indeed. The middle ward was built such that the walls and towers were actually part of the cliff face. It was too hard for the miners to get their picks into the rock, and the cat-apults, even mighty Cabulus, were ineffective against the solidity of these walls. The French were facing the daunting task of mounting a suicidal frontal attack using ladders and movable towers of their own.

Then one of the soldiers, Peter Bogis, noticed an opening built for garbage and waste, called a "garderobe," on the west side of the castle. With much excitement, Bogis realized that the opening was not barred, so he and a few fellow soldiers climbed up into this smelly, slippery opening. Incredibly, they soon found themselves inside the middle ward near the chapel.

8.2 Early French trebuchet.

Once inside, Bogis and the other soldiers came up with a plan. They decided to make noise, a lot of noise, in order to fool the English into thinking they were being overrun by a huge attacking force, already inside the middle ward. It worked. The English, thinking there were squads of French soldiers breaking in through the chapel, retreated again, this time towards the last and final refuge of Chateau Gaillard, the inner ward, or "castle keep." Now that the French were inside the middle ward, it was finally time to unleash the awesome power in Cabulus's mighty arm. The trebuchet was built from a lattice of heavy oak beams, as large and well constructed as an oil derrick. The cross arm was probably a structure made from several wood beams bolted together, with the grain of each beam oriented at cross angles to add strength. Attached to the short end of the cross arm was the counterweight, a very large wooden box full of thousands of pounds of rocks or lead weight.

8.3 Late French trebuchet.

To fire the weapon, the engine master ordered his crew to tug on ropes attached to blocks and tackles or heavy winches. "Heave!" cried the captain. "Heave again!" The heavy weight would rapidly gain elevation, and as it did so, the throwing end would lower closer and closer to the ground. When the counterweight was at full height, a stout pin was inserted into the framework to keep the counterweight in place.

A sling was then attached to the throwing end and a stone projectile placed within. When all was ready, the engine commander would take a sledgehammer and knock loose the holding pin. Down fell the weighted bucket, and up went the throwing arm, dragging the sling. The sling would snap forward, and at just the right angle, the projectile would leap free, flying far and true against the castle wall. Crash!

Quickly the mighty arm would be retracted again, and like the pit crew at a modern automobile race, each member of the firing crew would snap into action. Some would winch the arm down again, some would reload the sling with a stone, one would replace the pin. Crash! Reload. Crash! Reload.

The swinging arms of Cabulus and the other catapults set up a steady, whooshing rhythm as the slings whipped through the air. Ball after stone ball crashed against the walls. Rock chips flew immediately; soon cracks appeared in the wall, then finally large gaping holes.

The inner walls were no match for the horse catapult and its companions. Soon, the English knew there was no hope for holding the castle. On March 6, the last 120 knights and foot soldiers laid down their arms and surrendered.

While the siege of Chateau Gaillard would have a lasting effect on the relationship between England and France, it did not really shorten the Hundred Years War. In fact, it would be 350 more years until the last vestiges of English hegemony would be gone from the area we know today as France. But Cabulus proved that no castle could be considered impregnable from the big machines of an attacking army.

Cabulus, The Great Horse Trebuchet

Adult supervision required

 Use protective eyewear

Swinging arm alert: Watch out for moving arms or levers

Sharp and/or heavy tool advisory: Project requires use of saw or hammer

Flying object alert: Use care when aiming and firing

Now it's time to build a model of Cabulus, Philip Augustus's great castle-smashing trebuchet catapult. The model shown here is based on an actual fourteenth-century French design depicted in a manuscript found in the Bibliothèque Nationale de France, the French National Library. The ancient illustrated manuscript shows a large trebuchet made from a split log and powered by a counterweight.

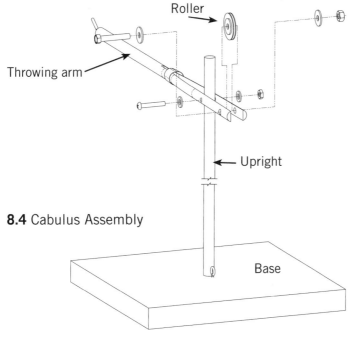

Roller

Throwing arm

Upright

8.4 Cabulus Assembly

Base

105

MATERIALS

- Saw
- Wire cutter
- Drill with a ⅝-inch bit and a ³⁄₁₆-inch bit
- String
- Counterweight (Any convenient object that weighs approximately ½ pound; a $10 roll of US quarters is about right.)
- Electrical or strapping tape
- Glue
- Pencil

Base

- (1) piece of 10-inch by 10-inch by 1-inch pine board
- (1) small eyescrew
- (1) release hook (⅛-inch-diameter wire, bent into a hook)

Upright

- (1) 17½-inch-long hardwood dowel, ½-inch diameter

Throwing Arm

- (1) #10-24 bolt, 1½ inches long, and nut
- (1) wooden or metal roller, approximately 1 to 1½ inches in diameter. (A roller is a wheel with a groove cut into the rolling surface. You can use a replacement roller for a patio or garage door, or make one out of a toy wooden wheel by cutting the groove yourself with the saw. If you cannot find or make a roller, you can omit it completely and let the rope simply hang over the bolt, although it won't work as well.)
- (1) ½-inch hex bolt 1½ inches long, and nut
- (1) 18-inch-long hardwood dowel, ½-inch diameter (Throwing Arm)
- (2) washers, for #10-24 bolts
- (2) washers, for ½-inch-diameter bolts
- (1) small wire nail or brad, 1 inch long

DIRECTIONS

1. Prepare the Base. Starting at one corner of the Base, draw a straight line to the opposite corner. Do the same thing between the two remaining corners. The intersection of the two lines is the center point of the board. Drill a ⅝-inch hole cleanly through the Base at this point.

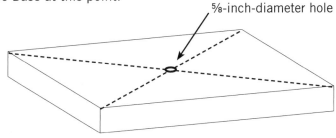

⅝-inch-diameter hole

8.5

2. Prepare the Upright. Drill a ³⁄₁₆-inch hole through the upright at a point 2 inches from one end.

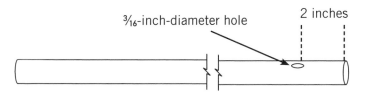

³⁄₁₆-inch-diameter hole   2 inches

8.6

3. Prepare the Throwing Arm. Drill a ³⁄₁₆-inch hole through the Throwing Arm at a point 10 inches from one end.

4. Saw the Throwing Arm exactly in half longitudinally, starting at the same end from which you measured the distance for the hole—the "reference end"—and in the same plane as the hole, through the center of the of the Throwing Arm to a point just short of the hole. This hole is there to prevent the wood from splitting. See the diagram for reference before you begin sawing.

    The long saw cut that this project requires means that a table saw would be preferred, but it is possible to make the required cuts with a hand saw if you work slowly and very, very carefully.

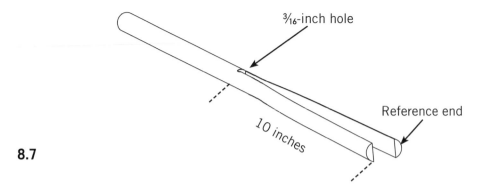

¾₁₆-inch hole

Reference end

10 inches

8.7

5. Drill two ³⁄₁₆-inch-diameter holes at 90 degrees to the saw cut on the Throwing Arm, one at a point ½ inch (Hole A) from the reference end, and the other 3½ inches (Hole B) from the reference end.

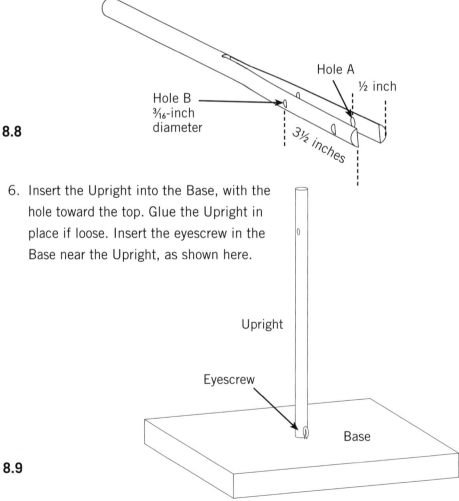

Hole A

½ inch

Hole B
³⁄₁₆-inch
diameter

8.8

3½ inches

6. Insert the Upright into the Base, with the hole toward the top. Glue the Upright in place if loose. Insert the eyescrew in the Base near the Upright, as shown here.

Upright

Eyescrew

Base

8.9

7. Gently separate the two sawn halves of the Throwing Arm and align the Throwing Arm Hole B with the hole in the Upright. Insert the #10-24 bolt with the #10 washers and gently tighten the nut.

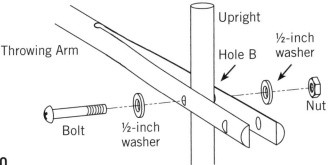

8.10

8. Place the roller between the sawn halves of the Throwing Arm and align Hole A with the roller. Insert the ½-inch hex bolt with the ½-inch washers and gently tighten the nut. You may add washers between the roller and the Throwing Arm if there is excessive play.

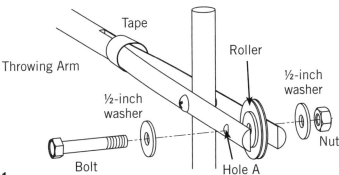

8.11

9. Reinforce the Throwing Arm with electrical or strapping tape as shown.

10. Insert a wire nail or brad into the non-cut end of the Throwing Arm. Use the wire cutter to cut off the end so there is only ½-inch of nail exposed. Gently bend the wire nail upward to an angle about 45 degrees up from alignment with the Throwing Arm.

11. Insert the eyescrew into the Base, 1 inch from the Upright, in the same direction as the short end of the Throwing Arm. (See **diagram 8.9** at Step 6.)

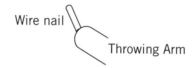

Wire nail

Throwing Arm

8.12

12. Attach the counterweight to the trebuchet by running a string from the eyescrew in the Base, up and over the roller to the hanging ½-pound weight as shown below.

Congratulations! Your medieval model trebuchet is ready to lay siege.

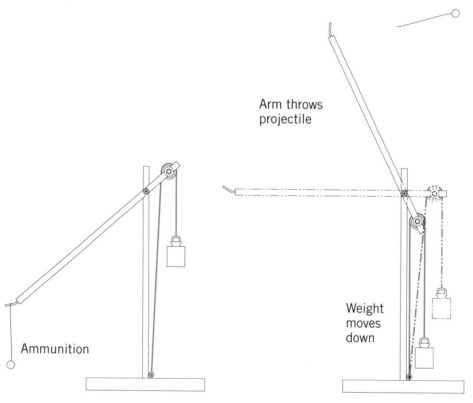

Arm throws projectile

Ammunition

Weight moves down

8.13

AMMUNITION AND OPERATING THE TREBUCHET

This trebuchet can throw a variety of things—walnuts, plastic cows, tiny barrels—it's really up to the master of engines. But, to get the best performance, you need to attach the ammunition to the trebuchet by a sling.

1. Tie one end of a piece of string in a loop. Tie the other end of the string to the object you desire to throw. Place the ammunition on the base and retract the sling as far as you can without letting the loop fall off the nail.

   How long should the sling be for optimal distance? That depends on several factors and makes for an interesting experiment. The velocity and acceleration relationship between the back end of the throwing arm, where the release hook is, and the sling is quite complicated and requires a lengthy college-physics-level discussion to explain. Instead of calculating the length, simply try slings cut from string of various lengths and see what happens. Start with a sling about the same size as the length between the release tip end and the pivot point.

2. To fire, pull the arm down to lift the counterweight. Let go and watch your trebuchet hurl its projectile up and away, lofting it high and far in a graceful parabolic arc toward the target.

THE MEDIEVAL CARPENTERS

Around the year 1300, a group of carpenters founded their own labor organization, a sort of medieval union, called the Carpenter's Guild. The guild still exists and is probably the oldest worker's organization in existence.

The incorporating papers of the guild includes the following:

> This is the Book of Ordinances of the Brotherhood of Carpenters of London made the first day of September, in the seventh year of the reign of our King Edward III after the Conquest.

The book of ordinances listed several rules and regulations for its members.

Each member was obliged to attend mass in midwinter, to pay dues amounting to one penny per man. Members had to attend funerals of deceased members, and through the guild provisions would be made to pay for services to the dead man's family. Sick members were assisted, as were those who were out of work. The guild was to be governed by four wardens, elected annually, who assessed dues four times a year.

It wasn't easy to get into the carpenter's guild, as many men would eagerly join such a well-paying and well-organized group. But those who did get in worked on their skills for years, starting first as apprentices, moving on to journeymen, and finally, if they were good enough, achieving the rank of master carpenters.

The guild members built houses, buildings, mills, and cathedrals; but nothing tested their skill and artistry more than building catapults. The carpenters had to endure battlefield conditions, sometimes dodging stones and arrows. A massive trebuchet could be seven stories high, and erecting such a massive structure without a crane was complex indeed. And to top it off, trebuchet builders didn't use a lot of nails, screws, and other modern fasteners. They used strong but complex wooden joints, cut right into the beams to hold them together without nails.

The techniques of the medieval carpenters for building the big siege engines of Richard and Philip Augustus are still practiced by modern-day craftsmen who call themselves "timber framers." Timber frame construction is a building technique that creates freestanding, self-supporting wood frames that are held together by wooden pegs. Each timber is cut to join with another so that they lock together. The joined timbers create a solid framework that does not require walls or metal fasteners for support.

THE FLOUR SACK THROWER OF GIBRALTAR

Gibraltar is a small peninsula off the coast of Spain known for its huge, imposing rock cliff and is one of the most frequently besieged places in all of Europe. Dozens of different nations, ranging from ancient Phoenicia to modern Great Britain have occupied the place, and nearly every change in ownership has resulted in a long siege. And, as you may have figured out by now, where there's a siege, there's very often a catapult.

THE 1333 SIEGE OF GIBRALTAR

In 1333, the Sultan of Morocco sent an army of 7,000 soldiers led by his son, Abu Malik, to attack the fortress of Gibraltar which was commanded by Don Vasco Perez de Meira, a Spanish knight in the employ of King Alfonso XI of Castile.

Unfortunately for Alfonso, Don Vasco was a lousy commander and more than a little corrupt, so the defenders of the fortress became increasingly undermanned, poorly equipped, and low on food. With great concern, the defenders could see a great number of Moorish troops take up positions surrounding the fortress and they knew they couldn't hold for long.

When news that Gibraltar was under attack reached King Alfonso, he was on the other side of the country and embroiled in other disputes which prevented him from immediately sending an army to relieve the fort. But he did get word to his admiral, Don Alonso Teorio, ordering him to move his fleet into position that he may assist Don Vasco in whatever way he could.

Admiral Teorio did not have enough soldiers to fight his way onto the Great Rock itself, but he was quite aware of the lack of food inside the beleaguered town. So, he ordered his men to build a group of large hurling machines and position them on the decks of the ships. Their purpose was not to toss rocks and stones at the Moors but instead to hurl sacks of flour into the besieged town to prevent the people there from starving.

But alas, Don Alonso was not much of a catapult builder. Most of the sacks wound up either in the ocean or in the hands of the Moors. The fortress garrison began to starve. In addition, the town itself had been badly battered and damaged by the constant assault from Moorish catapults. Unable to resist any longer, Don Vasco and the soldiers of Gibraltar surrendered.

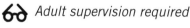

The Gibraltar-Style Catapult

👓 *Adult supervision required*

🪜 Swinging arm alert: Watch out for moving arms or levers

Sharp and/or heavy tool advisory: Project requires use of saw or hammer

Flying object alert: Use care when aiming and firing

The power behind this catapult's arm is a spring made from twisted rope. (The Spanish and Moors probably used linen and horsehair, but natural fibers like hemp and sisal, which stretch less than nylon rope, are also excellent for catapults.) Be aware that when it's fully wound up, the rope places immense stress on the entire structure, so it's important to build the wooden frame solidly. Without the pair of cross-braces, the machine could implode when the spring is tightened.

The tightened rope spring also makes it difficult to release the throwing arm. A little mechanical device called a panic snap, available at hardware stores, makes a fast, controllable trigger. It disconnects easily because its latching mechanism is separate from the load-bearing structure.

But even with a good trigger, hurling the ammo properly can be tricky—something you learn early on when figuring out how to build a catapult. Let go too early, and it shoots straight up. Too late, and it plows into the ground in front of you. Try attaching a cord to the projectile and then looping the other end around a peg in the top of the throwing arm. The longer the loop, the farther a missile will fly.

You may not wish to utilize your catapult for warfare, but you might try flinging baseballs or (well wrapped) burritos. Such tactics may not win any battles against the attacking armies—but you will have a lot more fun.

You have a lot of leeway as to how to build your catapult. The drawings and instructions that follow will provide you with important pieces of information, but quite likely you'll still need to figure out some of the dimensions on your own. However, that's okay because this is a DIY project—tweaking it is part of the fun of making it.

MATERIALS

- (2) 2-inch x 4-inch boards, 33 inches long*
- (2) 4-inch x 4-inch boards, 15 inches long
- (4) 2-inch x 4-inch boards, 17 inches long
- (1) 2-inch x 4-inch boards, 15 inches long
- (1) 1½-inch-diameter round dowel, 26 inches long
- (3) ½-inch-diameter dowels, 3 inches long
- (20) ⁵⁄₁₆-inch lag screws, 3 inches long
- (1) 2-inch-long finish nail
- (1) Panic snap
- (1) Large eyescrew (to attach panic snap to frame)
- (1) Large eyescrew (to attach panic snap to throwing arm)
- (2) 3-inch steel lazy susan turntables, optional (Internet search term: "3 inch lazy susan")
- (4) 3-, 4-, or 5- inch plate casters (optional)
- (2) lag screws, 4 inches long
- (2) lag screws 5 inches long
- 25 feet of rope
- Drill
- 2½-inch hole saw
- ½-inch wood bit
- ¼-inch bit
- Ratchet or wrench set
- Hammer
- 2 feet of cord or twine
- Projectile (like an old tennis ball)

*If desired, you can use good-quality cedar boards instead of pine because they weather well and look authentic, but any type of softwood will be fine.

1. Build a sturdy wooden frame, using **diagrams 9.1** and **9.2** as guides. Use a hole saw to drill a 2½ inch hole in each 2 x 6 as shown in **diagram 9.1**. Attach the turntable if you choose on the outboard side of each hole with the screws that come with it.

Then use the lag screws to attach the 15-inch 4 x 4 crosspieces to the two 33-inch long 2 x 6 boards. Drill a ¼-inch pilot hole for each lag screw before tightening them with the ratchet or wrench.

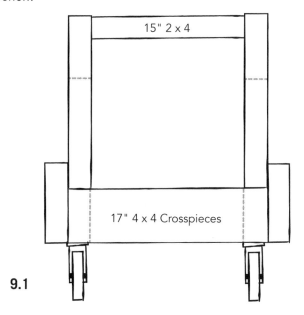

9.1

2. Use two 3-inch lag bolts to attach the two 17-inch long 2 x 4s in an upright position relative to the interior of the 2 x 6 frame pieces. Refer to **diagrams 9.1** and **9.2** for correct positioning.

3. Cut 45 degree angles on the remaining 17-inch long 2 x 4s as shown. Use 3-inch lag bolts to connect these pieces to frame and uprights frame with two screws for each connection. To attach the angled support pieces to the upright pieces, you'll need a couple of 4-inch and a couple of 5-inch lag screws.

4. Place a piece of foam padding on the top crosspiece to cushion the impact of the throwing arm.

5. Wheels are optional. The plate casters mount to the front and back crosspieces, but if you choose, you can forgo mobility and opt for solid wood blocks instead.

6. Attach an eyescrew to the throwing arm and pound a 2-inch finish nail in the center of the dowel throwing arm's top surface. Attach a panic snap to the top of the rear crosspiece, in the center.

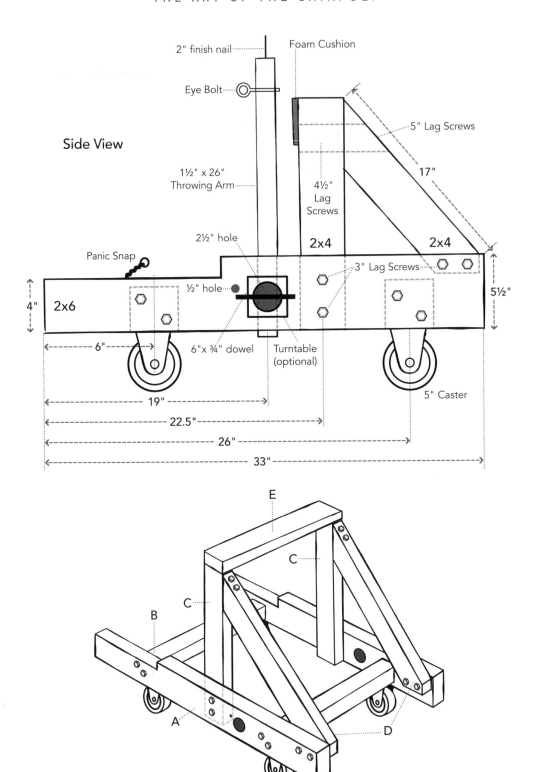

Side View

2" finish nail

Foam Cushion

Eye Bolt

5" Lag Screws

1½" x 26"
Throwing Arm

17"

4½"
Lag
Screws

2x4

2x4

2½" hole

Panic Snap

3" Lag Screws

½" hole

5½"

4"

2x6

6"

6"x ¾" dowel

Turntable
(optional)

5" Caster

19"

22.5"

26"

33"

E

C

C

B

A

D

9.2 Frame assembly diagram

7. The catapult's power comes from a skein of rope which is in reality, a torsion spring. Drill ½-inch diameter holes for the "stop dowels" just to the side of the turntables as shown.

8. As shown in **diagram 9.3**, wrap the rope tightly over and over between the ⅝-inch dowels and tie it off when you run out of rope. Optionally, you can place steel turntables between the side of the 2 x 6 pieces and the ⅝-inch-diameter dowel. The turntables have ball bearings, and they reduce the friction between the dowel and the onager's sides so you can add more twist to the rope skein.

9. Insert the throwing arm through the center of the skein and then rotate the pegs in the direction opposite to the flight of the projectile. This tensions the spring. The more you twist, the farther the projectile will travel, but here's a warning: too much tension may break the pegs, or even the frame.

9.3

Your catapult is ready to fling tennis balls, flour sacks, or just about anything else you can think of!

To fire the catapult, attach your projectile to a short length of cord (experiment to find the length that works the best) and tie a loop in the opposite end of the rope. Push the throwing arm down so it rests against the rear crosspiece. Place the projectile loop over the nail on the top of the throwing arm and attach the panic snap to the eye-screw on the throwing arm. Stand well clear of the rotational axis of the throwing arm. Then pull down on the panic snap collar to fire.

9.4

KEEPING SAFETY IN MIND

1. Watch your hands and fingers! If you put them in the wrong place, they could get pinched.
2. The areas in back of and in front of the catapult are danger zones! Keep hands, heads, and the rest of your body away from the Throwing Arm whenever there is tension in the rope spring. Keep the area in front and in back of the catapult clear.
3. Choose sensible projectiles and be aware of the range of your machine.

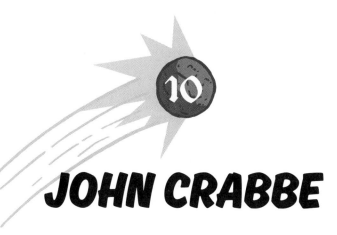

JOHN CRABBE

TINKERER, SAILOR, SOLDIER, SPY

In the year of our Lord 1340, and in the fourteenth year of his reign, our Lord King Edward III of England observed the feast of Pentecost at Ipswich in preparation for his crossing into Flanders with a small following. But he soon heard that the king of France was planning to impede his crossing by dispatching a fleet of ships from Spain, in addition to the entire French navy, so our king summoned ships from all over England until he had a with him 260 ships, both large and small.

So begins an important part of the Chronicle of Galfridi Le Baker de Swynebroke, a medieval historian better known in his day as Jeffrey the Baker. He was an English chronicler who probably lived in Oxfordshire, a small town in England, between the years 1300 and 1360. In Jeffrey's time, England and France were engaged in a long bitter war—so long in duration, in fact, that historians refer to it as "the Hundred Years War."

In June of 1340 the English decided to attack the French fleet. The French fleet was under the command of Admiral Hugues Quierat, and the English navy engaged them in the sea just off the town of

Sluys, a trading port in Holland. The naval battle raged for a full nine hours. The English and French ships engaged each other in close combat, a savage type of fighting that included archer attacks at first, and after the ships got close together, hand-to-hand fighting with swords, pikes, and even clubs.

As it turned out, the English fleet bested the French forces. The chroniclers of the time, like Jeffrey the Baker, tell us that close to 30,000 men died, mostly Frenchmen, but most people who read such figures suspect them to be very much exaggerated.

During the height of the battle Edward sent one of his best naval commanders, a man named John Crabbe, into the fray with a fleet of 40 warships in order to pursue the fleeing French fleet. (Try to say "fleeing French fleet" three times really fast!) Crabbe and his men captured several French ships—the *Denis,* the *George,* the *Christopher,* and the *Black Rooster.* All told, John Crabbe and the English captured over 200 French ships. The result of the battle of Sluys was that it put an end to the threat of a French invasion of the English mainland. From that point on, all the warfare associated with the Hundred Years War would take place in France, not England.

It is interesting that one of Edward's best admirals wasn't an Englishman at all, but a Fleming (Fleming means "a person from Flanders," the area where Belgium and parts of the Netherlands and Northern France are today). This remarkable man was John Crabbe. During his life, Crabbe was first a pirate, then a sailor, then a merchant, but most of all, he was a master builder of catapults.

THE GANG FROM OOSTBURG

Most historians, even those who specialize in the time period surrounding the Hundred Years War between England and France, are unfamiliar with John Crabbe. But Crabbe was quite a colorful character, moving between Flanders, England, Scotland, and France, working at one time for the Duke of Flanders, the next year for England's Edward II, the next for Louis of France, and then back again to someone else. For Crabbe was a swashbuckling pirate and a man of aristocratic sensibilities, a man who sailed the high seas and attended the royal courts of Europe with equal ease, finding loot and plunder in both locations alike.

In the year 1305 Crabbe sat down with his friends in the Flemish town of Oostburg, and they began to plot. In a meeting with his friends Milo de Uteham, Christian Tobbying, John Labban, and the mysterious young relative of Crabbe's, known only as "the Crabbekyn," they decided to sail the high seas, finding rich, fat, and lightly armed merchant ships, which they would rob and plunder.

Piracy on the high seas had been common since the days of the ancient Greeks; it was dangerous, violent, and brutal. But John Crabbe had an idea, one that would make him famous as both a pirate and a tinkerer. For in those days gunpowder was not yet used in Europe. There were no cannons, no rifles, no guns of any kind. If you were a pirate bent on robbing a merchant ship, you had to sail next to it, and your men would have to jump aboard, brandishing their swords and spears. If the men of the unlucky vessel would not give up, then fighting hand to hand with the desperate sailors was the only alternative if you were serious about getting booty.

Crabbe, the intellectual pirate, had a better idea. Why not, he thought, build and mount specially designed naval catapults on his pirate ship, catapults capable of pounding stone balls through the decks of merchant ships, and capable of shooting iron-tipped darts through the walls and hulls of ships? A terrific idea, thought Crabbe and his gang, and his men sailed their ship from Muiden, Flanders, in search of action.

They soon found it. A few days out from Muiden, from the crow's nest high above the deck, the young Crabbekyn saw sails on the horizon and shouted down to his friends, "*Ik zien de schip!* (I see a ship!)"

Crabbekyn had spotted the *Waardebourc*, a merchant ship laden with tons of valuable cargo, including cloth, wool, and most valuable of all, wine. The Oostburg Gang heaved to and soon their pirate ship was brought broadside, next to the unlucky Flemish cargo ship.

There was terror in the eyes of the men under attack. They could see the terrible machines on deck, and they feared what those machines could and would do. Here, in the middle of the Bay of Biscay, far from land, the *Waardebourc* was under attack from catapults! Crabbe's men loaded and fired, reloaded and refired. Time and again the pirates loaded missiles into the catapult slings and raised the counterweight. Time and again, the counterweight swung down, launching a barrage of deadly missiles that pounded the innocent trading ship. The sailors cowered, trying to keep from being smashed to death by incoming rocks and darts. The Gang was relentless, and so the rocks and arrows flew, punching holes in the deck and peppering the hull with punctures from the javelins and arrows from the war engines. The *Waardebourc* was defenseless. The Gang could blast away with trebuchets and ballistae at will, and it soon became apparent to all that just a few more well-placed shots would certainly sink the ship.

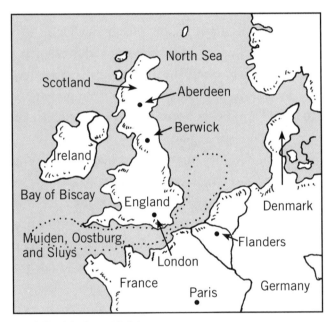

10.1 Map of Crabbe's activities.

The captain of the doomed ship gave up. The pirates climbed aboard and took all the goods—including 160 "tunnes" or large casks of wine. The pirates commandeered the ship and took the sailors captive. Then, for no particular reason except that this is what pirates sometimes do, they torched the ship and it sunk to the bottom of the sea.

For a few more years the gang sailed the sea, robbing ships and looting, and selling the stolen cargo in the trading ports of Flanders.

Then the gang from Oostburg struck the big time by attacking an English ship, one that was loaded with more than just wine and cloth: this one held gold, silver, and jewels. The catapult raiders hit the jackpot with this raid, and this made them "hot property" indeed. They decided it was time to lay low for a while. The English king and his navy were looking hard for the Catapult Pirates, and Crabbe certainly did not want to receive the kind of brutal justice that captured pirate captains normally received, such as imprisonment or even hanging.

So around 1310 he left the high seas and took refuge from English justice by settling in with the longtime enemy of the English, the Scots. Apparently Mr. Crabbe had found the city of Aberdeen, Scotland, much to his liking, and it really was a good choice. Like Crabbe, there were a number of Flemish merchants, rogues, and pirates who settled in Scotland because they found it profitable to prey on English shipping, plunder the English ships on the high seas, sell the stolen goods in the Flemish ports of Amsterdam and Antwerp, and then return to Scotland, protected by the Scottish crown.

For the next several years, the catapult pirate John Crabbe and his band maintained a busy schedule as freebooters, plundering English shipping and making quite a comfortable livelihood for themselves. He enjoyed living in Scotland. And, in addition to being a most clever pirate, he was a shrewd political animal. He took great advantage of the constant warring between Scotland and England, which made it possible for him to be a pirate as well as an important and valued Scottish businessman.

In 1318 Crabbe moved from Aberdeen to Berwick, another town in Scotland. There Crabbe showed how useful the construction skills he learned building catapults and rigging sails would be. Crabbe started to build enormous land-based catapults for the Scottish chieftains.

In 1318 and 1319 the English army marched on Scotland, trying to conquer the Scots and spread English hegemony over all of the island of Britain. The castle located at the town of Berwick in Scotland was the scene of several important battles and sieges between the Scots and the English. Around 1296 King Edward I, in one of the many battles that earned him the nickname "Hammer of the Scots," led his troops in a fight that resulted in English control of Berwick and the important castle there. But the relations between the Scots and the English continued to be very bad, and for the next hundred years the castle was the scene of regular battles for control and power.

In 1318 the Scots besieged Berwick Castle, then held by the English. The attack was vigorous and bloody, and when it was over Berwick was Scottish again. Scotland's leader, the famous Robert the Bruce, gave command of the castle to a trusted castellan named Walter Steward. The English were not willing to give up Berwick without a good long fight, and Walter knew he had his hands full.

Outside the castle walls, the English army massed. Archers, knights, men of war were crowding outside the gates. The English had siege towers and miners, and they had trebuchets—massive ones that could fling 300-pound stones capable of crumbling even Berwick's thick stone walls. Steward turned to his acquaintance, a Flemish merchant who lived nearby, a man with a rather checkered past. That man was our friend, the former pirate, who had risen to become a burgess or respected merchant—John Crabbe.

Crabbe, the master catapult builder, got down to work. He decided to defend Scotland by fighting fire with fire. He started to design and build trebuchets with enough power and accuracy to hit and destroy England's own catapults. His building crews worked round the clock. And they were successful. There is a very important history written by a man named John Barbour, who lived in Scotland during this time period. Barbour is considered the father of medieval Scottish literature, and he wrote a long account of the Battle of Berwick. Here is an excerpt from his famous book The Bruce, written in the ancient language of Scotland called Old Scots in which he describes the machines and deeds of Crabbe.

> John Crab, a Flemyne (Fleming), als had he
> That we of gret subtilite
> Till ordane (ordered) til make aparale (equipment) For till
> defend and till assale (attack)
> Castell (castle) of wer othan cite (city) That nane slear
> mycht (power) fundin be

> He gert (caused) engyins (catapults) and trammys ma
> And purvait (provided) gree fyre (fire) alsua
> Spryngaldis (a catapult) and schotis (catapult) on sier
> manneris
> That till defend castell.

Can you understand the writing of a fourteenth-century Scottish poet? Certainly, these lines are very difficult for modern English speakers to read! But if you puzzle them out, you can get a good feel that John Crabbe was thought to be a military man of great skill and exceptional cleverness, and that the siege engines he built led the defense of the castle.

During the siege of Berwick, Barbour tells us that the Scots, under Crabbe's direction, built a number of large catapults and siege engines for the defense of the castle. The Scots gathered barrels of pitch and tar, set them ablaze, and shot the burning barrels towards the English and their catapults.

England launched a desperate frontal assault on the castle using scaling ladders, but they were beaten back. It must have been a very tough fight, as Barbour writes that during the press of battle the blows from both sides left "sum ded, sum hurt, and sum swavnand. Bot thai that held on fut in hy, and skunnyrrit thar for nakyn" ("some were dead, some were hurt, and some left swooning. But those that held on fought with vigor and retreated not at all").

The English then built a movable battering ram called a "sow" and brought it up against the castle walls. The ram started to pound the walls. For a time the outcome of the siege of Berwick was up for grabs, but the chroniclers tell us that "John Crabbe himself had all his gear ready, for up on the castle walls, he was able to rain down fire upon it until it was burnt up." So ended the Siege of Berwick, in a draw. The wars between the English and the Scottish went on for years. In 1327 there are more historical records showing Crabbe making a lucrative income building catapults for the Scottish royalty.

In 1332 Crabbe led a flotilla, or fleet, of 10 Scottish warships against the English, but this time the luck of the catapult pirate ran out. The English fleet routed the attackers and sank all 10 ships in

Crabbe's fleet. Crabbe made his escape and managed to find his way back to Berwick, but he was soon captured by supporters of the English side. This was a real prize of war, and Crabbe was soon brought before the king himself. Somehow, some way, the daring Fleming talked the English into not only sparing his life, but giving him a post of importance with the English navy, building (what else?) catapults for them. The defender of the Scots had gone over to the other side. The Scots were beside themselves with anger at Crabbe. They said he was a traitor, a turncoat, and even a spy!

For the rest of his life, Crabbe worked for the English, leading sailors to battle against the French and supplying the English with the munitions and ancient artillery that made them the greatest sea power in the world.

KNOWING THE ROPES

There is no material as important to the good working of a siege engine as rope. Ropes were used to pull back the counterweights on Crabbe's trebuchets, and they pulled back the mighty bows of Alexander's ballistae. They were employed on the ancient cranes used to erect the tall perriers of France. They were the material from which the onager's powerful torsion spring was made. And when 25 Chinese or Arab soldiers pulled together in a mighty tug to fling the stones in their traction catapults, what did they pull on? Ropes!

The ropes used in catapults have been made from many different materials over time. Natural fibers derived from the sinewy parts of plant stalks and leaves have been used to make rope since ancient times. The very best catapult ropes were thought to be made from animal tendons called sinews, but other materials, such as hair, were also used. The classical writer and catapult expert Vitruvius says in his writing that both animal hair and sinew make excellent catapult ropes, although he indicates that, of all possibilities, catapult ropes made from women's hair are the very best. Other ancient writers disagree. The Roman military expert Vegetius strongly endorses the use of sinew from the neck of an ox for use in artillery; to him, hair from the manes and tails of horses is merely a useful substitute, but he does agree that women's hair is excellent in an emergency.

Making Rope

Here's an experiment that shows how the men who built catapults for John Crabbe made rope.

MATERIALS

- Cotton balls
- Pencil or small stick

DIRECTIONS

1. Take a large cotton ball and pull out some cotton fibers. Observe how easily the cotton fibers break apart; each individual cotton fiber is thin and weak.

10.2

2. Now pull out a few fibers from the clump in the cotton ball with your right hand (you use your left if you are left-handed), slowly and with slight tension, twisting the fibers between your thumb and forefinger.

10.3

3. Try to break the twisted fibers by pulling on them. If you did this right, you will notice that the rope formed is much harder to break! It is the twist in a rope that gives the rope its strength.

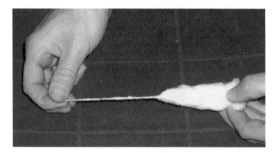

10.4

4. Gently and slowly pull out some more fibers from the cotton ball, and continue to twist them up. You can simply rub the cotton down your thigh to quickly twist the fibers if you want.
5. Wind the twisted fibers around the middle of a pencil or stick. This will allow you to hold the twist while you continue to lengthen your rope.

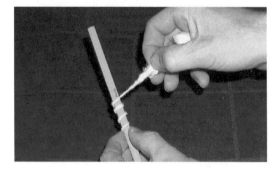

10.5

6. Keep pulling fibers out of the cotton ball slowly and evenly, while twisting the pen or stick. That's it—you have a made a rope!

If you practice long enough, you will be able to make a rope of considerable length and strength. You can use the rope as a sling, or perhaps as part of the torsion spring on the ballista or mangonel.

Spring Engine Catapult

Adult supervision required

6ð Use protective eyewear

✗ Sharp and/or heavy tool advisory: Project requires use of saw or hammer

● Flying object alert: Use care when aiming and firing

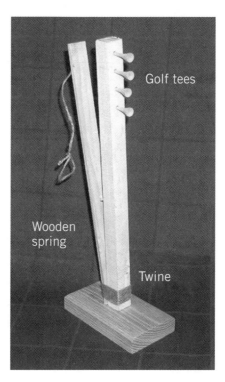

3.5
Spring
Engine

Catapult historians sometimes describe a very simple type of catapult that uses a flexible arm to smack an arrow or bunch of arrows toward the enemy. These devices have been called l'espringales, or springalds, but usually they are simply referred to as spring engines.

Of all the catapults, spring engines such as these are among the very oldest. They are the simplest catapults to build and use and relatively cheap to produce. Because they are so simple, it is likely that peoples before the ancient Greeks used such devices, although no definitive proof, such as pictures or written records, exists. However, if made well, spring engines could be very effective, especially in the beginning of a pitched battle. The spring engine was capable of shooting a shower of poorly aimed but extremely numerous arrows or javelins all at once.

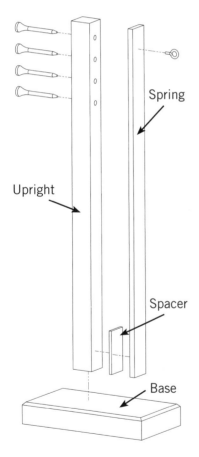

Although it is called a spring engine, there is no metal coil spring in it. Instead, the spring is a simple but very large flat wooden arm. When the flat arm is flexed by pulling one end back, great tension builds up in the fibers of the wood, and it snaps back with great force when released. Usually, the springs were made from several thin wooden boards glued together to make a massive, yet pliable, wooden spring. Pulling back such a spring would take many men or a winch-like device. After the spring was pulled back, it was held back with a metal pin. When it was time to fire, the soldier in charge of the catapult would knock the pin out with a hammer or mallet and the great wooden spring would snap forward. As it did so, it would smack into the arrows or darts held in the upright and shoot them forward.

The following project shows you how to make a model spring engine that shoots a number of golf tees simultaneously. The golf

3.6 Spring Engine Assembly

tees don't shoot particularly far, but the spring engine is dependable, easy to make, and fun to use.

Be careful when shooting the spring engine. Do not aim at anyone and make certain that you don't pull back on the spring so far that it breaks.

MATERIALS

The Base

- (1) 4-inch by 6-inch piece of wood, 1 inch thick

The Upright

- (1) 16-inch piece of 1-inch by 1-inch square wooden dowel (any approximately 1-inch by 1-inch piece of wood, 16 inches long will work)

The Spacer

- (1) 1-inch by 2-inch piece of wood, ⅛ inch thick

The Spring

- (1) 1-inch by ½-inch piece of wood, 16 inches long

Miscellaneous

- Drill
- (1) small eyescrew
- (4) golf tees. If small children will be using this device, remove sharp ends from the tees.
- (1) ¼-inch-diameter wooden dowel, 1 inch long
- Glue
- String

DIRECTIONS

1. Drill a ¼-inch hole through the center of the Base. Drill a corresponding ¼-inch hole, ½-inch deep, in the bottom end of the Upright dowel as shown.

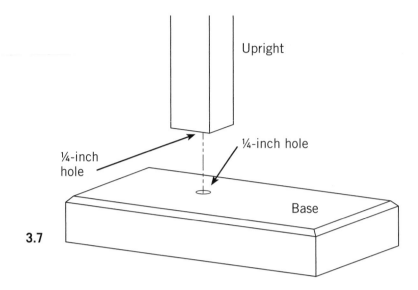

Upright

¼-inch hole

¼-inch hole

Base

3.7

2. Drill four ³⁄₁₆-inch-diameter holes through the top of the Upright as shown.

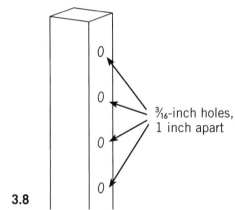

³⁄₁₆-inch holes, 1 inch apart

3.8

3. Glue the Spacer to the bottom face of the Upright as shown. Let dry.

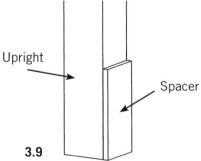

Upright

Spacer

3.9

4. Attach the small eyescrew to the Spring, near the top.

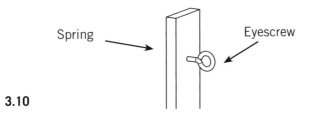

Spring   Eyescrew

3.10

5. Place a small amount of glue in the end hole in the Upright and in the hole in the Base. Connect the Upright to the Base by inserting the 2-inch-long, ½-inch-diameter dowel in the Base and Upright. Align the Upright and Base so all edges are square and the four upper holes in the Upright are aligned with the narrow end of the Base. Let dry.

6. Attach the Spring to the Upright by placing the Spring next to the Spacer glued to the Upright. Loop the string multiple times around the Base of the Upright and Spring and pull it tight. Tie off the string.

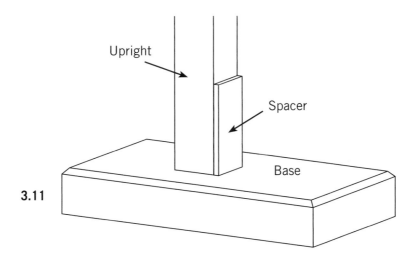

Upright

Spacer

Base

3.11

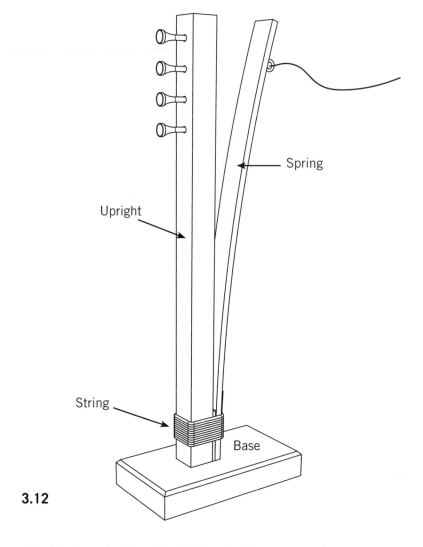

3.12

7. Attach a short length of string to the eyescrew to act as a pull cord.

OPERATING THE SPRING ENGINE

1. Pull back on the drawstring. You may have to have another person hold the Base in place.
2. Place one golf tee in each of the four holes. The end of the golf tees must extend out through the holes, such that when the Spring is released, it will hit the ends smartly.
3. Release the Spring and watch the golf tees shoot out.

KEEPING SAFETY IN MIND

The general safety rules described earlier must be followed. The Spring Engine is designed to shoot golf tees a short distance. Always keep the well-being of yourself and those around you in mind. Do not shoot any projectile at people or items that could break. Adult supervision is required and safety glasses are recommended.

11

THE HAMMER OF THE SCOTS

Early in the first millennium, an unknown Chinese engineer designed the first gravity-powered throwing machine. It used a long lever attached to a counterweight to toss a stone in a high, long arc. Unlike a ballista or mangonel, this type of catapult was often built on a very large scale, and so the rocks it threw could weigh as much as half a ton, sometimes even heavier.

To make it bigger and more powerful, the catapult designer simply needed to use thicker and longer timbers for the frame. There were no tricky torsion springs to wind, no complex release mechanisms to design. It was simply a matter of cutting and fitting long, strong beams to form a long lever, with an ammunition holder at one end and a box of heavy weights at the other.

The Chinese inventor called his machine "The Whirlwind." Some scholars say that Chinese catapults were common by the second century BCE, others say they were invented later than that. In any event, whirlwind technology remained a Chinese secret for several hundred years. The Chinese could throw stones as heavy as a man over 300 feet. They were able to throw flaming barrels of oil and pitch, arrows, and finally gunpowder-based explosives at their enemies.

Chinese ships armed with catapults set out to invade Japan in the thirteenth century. But the ships never reached Japan because they were stopped by a sudden storm—one that the Japanese were certain was foretold and sent by heaven. They gave this storm the name "kamikaze"—the divine wind.

But few good ideas can stay secret for too long, and by the year 1000, the gravity-powered catapult had made its way to the Middle East. The Turks and Arabs made improvements to the Asian design and called their gravity engines "the rope-haired witch." Finally, the medieval Europeans got a look at Arab catapult technology during the time of the Crusades. Soon the gravity-powered catapult, now called by its European name, "trebuchet," came into its own as the main type of European siege artillery. By the year 1300, military engineers all over Europe were building gravity-powered trebuchets. Now the strong castles that once made princes and kings close to invincible were vulnerable—vulnerable to attack by catapult.

"IT ISN'T OVER UNTIL I SAY IT'S OVER!"

In 1304, possibly the largest concentration of big trebuchet-type catapults ever seen in one place was assembled on the plains before the walls of Stirling Castle in Scotland. Stirling Castle is a large fortress, built and rebuilt many times over the centuries of warfare between the Scots and the English. It is situated high on a long-dead volcanic stump of black basaltic rock, overlooking the valley of the River Forth. The location is a very important one, as it guards the main north-south and east-west routes across Scotland. To control Stirling Castle is to control the crossroads of Scotland.

As it is located so strategically, the castle played a frequent role in the Scottish struggle against English domination. Around the turn of the fourteenth century, King Edward I of England, grandnephew of Richard the Lionheart, was intensely and relentlessly engaged in the activities that would earn him his nickname "Edward, Scottorum-Malleus," which means "Edward, Hammer of the Scots." Edward was a warrior king, a brilliant tactician, and a man who knew the value of using the latest technology to his advantage.

In Edward's medieval English army there were several important positions apart from soldier-at-arms and knight. When Edward's armies fought, as they did frequently at widely dispersed locations throughout Wales, France, and Scotland, they did so with a contingent of supporters—blacksmiths, woodcutters, armorers, wagoneers, woodcutters, pioneers (here, pioneer means a man who acted as scout and wayfinder), and most relevant to this history, engineers. Although most contemporary accounts barely mention the supporting auxiliaries, there is no doubt that Edward's military success was due in no small measure to their important efforts.

Take, for example, Edward's campaign against the Scots that occurred in the decades on either side of the year 1300. The Scots were fiercely independent; and as long as they were unconquered, the Scots would stay a thorn, an ache, or even worse in Edward's side. So Edward and the mighty English army went north to pacify the country and subjugate the unruly and recalcitrant Scots once and for all.

There were a series of sieges and pitched battles between Edward and the Scots, led by Robert the Bruce, William Wallace, and others. The names and places of the battles are famous in both English and Scottish history: Stirling Bridge, Bannockburn, Falkirk. In terms of catapults, though, one battle stands out: the Battle of Stirling Castle.

Thirteen of the most powerful trebuchet-style catapults were erected on the plain below Stirling Castle under Edward's direct orders. Their purpose was straightforward: they were to be used to break down the protective walls of mighty Stirling Castle, the last redoubt of Scottish independence, and allow Edward's archers and pikemen to take the castle once and for all. In the spring of 1304, the huge trebuchets were erected outside the castle walls under the dismayed and anxious gaze of the Scots' garrison inside. First the trebuchet called Robinette was set up, then the Gloucester was built, and after that the Segrave. Then, urged on by Edward's impatient directives, the corps of engineers, carpenters, and laborers worked week in and week out to assemble the rest of the massive, powerful trebuchets.

There were medieval-style cranes and gin poles that were used for placing beams and cross members, which the carpenters fashioned together with crude but sturdy wooden joinery. Train-car–sized rock holders were riveted together by the smiths. The wagoneers and the pioneers brought cartload after cartload of wood and stone to the building site. As the craftsmen erected the machines under the watchful direction of the siege engine master, called the "engynour" (from which the modern term engineer comes), the scene around Stirling Castle looked as busy as any modern-day construction site.

The other trebuchets were erected at the very walls of the Castle, one by one, their rather gentle-sounding names belying their power and destructive purposes—the Parson, the Forester, the Belfry, the Vicar, and the Verney. But the biggest and most awesome machines were erected last, and these hurling engines had the horsepower to fling projectiles that could destroy castle walls 12 feet thick. Capable of casting stones weighing as much as a small tractor, they were known as the Bad Neighbor, Tout Le Monde, and the most famous and the biggest of all, Ludgar the War Wolf.

Records of the time show that a man named Master Reginald was the engineer in charge of all the engines. Since he was in charge and represented the King's treasury, he carefully checked in the materials required to build the machines. Each cartload of siege engine raw materials that the wagoneers brought in was inspected, recorded in a journal, and paid for.

Some of the records and papers concerning the catapults constructed for this siege still exist. Sixteen wooden beams for the engine Forester, inspected and approved. Lead weights for the Segrave's counterweight, weighed and approved. Cables, ropes, pulleys, horsehides, leather for slings—Master Reginald kept records and papers for all of them. The construction continued at a rapid pace.

But as fast as Reginald and his men worked, it wasn't fast enough to suit impatient King Edward. He sent other men to nearby cities to hasten the flow of supplies. The King's clerks went scrambling to the cities of Inverness, Edinburgh, Blackness, and Linlithgow in an effort to get more supplies and get them sent to Stirling more quickly. The effort paid off. In an astoundingly short time, many of the massed engines were ready to go. By Easter, the artillery barrage began. By June, all of the trebuchets save the gigantic War Wolf were operating.

The siege lasted from April 22 to July 20, 1304. This is a surprisingly long time for the castle garrison to hold out considering the size and resources of the besieging English forces. The smaller catapults worked day and night battering the walls and hurling jars of burning oil over the castle walls, but the Scots remained defiant.

Finally, in July, Ludgar, King Edward's nickname for the War Wolf, was ready for action. The English army eagerly looked forward to seeing what this massive artillery piece could do. Even Edward's wife, Margaret of France, watched Ludgar's attack from a tower with a viewing balcony specially ordered by Edward.

Unfortunately for Edward and the other men anticipating a spectacle, the Scots had had enough. Like the other trebuchets, Ludgar was constructed plainly and purposefully in their view. And Ludgar the War Wolf, by all accounts, was enormous. The Scots could see the gigantic beams and baskets being winched into place. They could see the 300-pound stone balls being arrayed for use against them as ammunition. They held council and talked it over, desperately seeking any possible way out, any way of escape. Finally they came to the obvious conclusion—they couldn't outlast the English, not with Ludgar, the War Wolf, and his mechanical friends pitching rocks at them all day and all night, and they couldn't get past the surrounding English army. So they raised the white flag and sent a messenger with an offer of surrender to Edward.

Not so fast, replied Edward. Edward had spent lots of time and lots of effort on Ludgar and he wanted to see something for his money. Edward ripped up the surrender document and ordered the unfortunate Scots back inside Stirling Castle. The siege was taken up again. With its first toss, Ludgar broke down an entire castle wall, crumbling it like a broken clay pot. The next tosses fell upon the buildings inside the castle ward and collapsed them into wreckage and debris. This bombardment went on for a long while. Finally, with the castle reduced to rubble, Edward accepted the Scottish surrender. At the end of the siege only 30 men were left, and Edward spared their lives.

HOW TREBUCHETS WORK

The ancient Greeks wrote that all machines, no matter how big and complicated, were really made up from just a handful of the most simple and basic machine types. These basic machines, called "the simple machines," were the lever, the wheel and axle, the screw, the inclined plane, the pulley, and the wedge. Even something as complicated as a ballista, or, in our time, a bicycle or a cement mixer or even an automobile, could be ultimately broken down into basic parts that were one or another of these basic forms. The trebuchet is a complex machine based primarily on one simple machine, the lever.

How does this make a trebuchet different from the other types of catapults? After all, it is a machine built for throwing rocks and other missiles, just like a ballista or an onager. But unlike those types of catapults, which use the energy in a bent bow or coiled rope spring to launch the missile, the trebuchet works on a different principle altogether: A lever allows you to substitute force for speed and vice versa. For example, if you want to move a heavy rock by hand, you would have to get your arms around it and then lift with enough strength to pick it up. But, if instead of lifting it, you inserted a metal bar underneath it and then placed another rock underneath the lever as a pivot or fulcrum, you could apply much less force but apply it through a longer distance in order to get the rock to move. While you're working the lever, your hand is moving down at a faster speed than the rock is moving up; but the rock does move, and the lever still provides an easier way to move the rock. And this is exactly how a trebuchet works. A trebuchet is really just a big lever that allows either people or heavy weights to move rocks with enough speed to make them fly through the air.

In order to get the end of the trebuchet holding the missile to move, you need to apply a force to the other end. In the diagram, if we apply a force of, say, 10 pounds downward and clockwise, then the end with the rockholder that is farther away will move up and counterclockwise if the rock doesn't weigh more than 2 pounds. This is because the diagram shows that the rock-holder is five times farther away than the point where we apply the downward force.

And, because the rockholder is five times farther away, it moves five times faster than the downward applied force. Engineers would call this gain "mechanical advantage," and it is the reason the trebuchet can fling rocks so far. If we pull down on the lever at a rate of 10 feet per second, the rock is shot upwards at a rate of 50 feet per second. That's quite a gain in velocity!

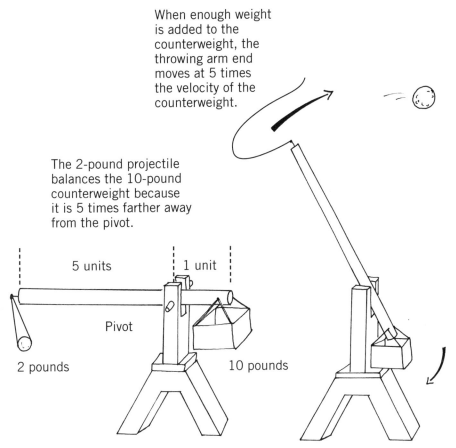

When enough weight is added to the counterweight, the throwing arm end moves at 5 times the velocity of the counterweight.

The 2-pound projectile balances the 10-pound counterweight because it is 5 times farther away from the pivot.

5 units

1 unit

Pivot

2 pounds

10 pounds

11.1 How a trebuchet works.

Ludgar the War Wolf was a well-designed trebuchet. Although Master Reginald and the other catapult masters left us no drawings or models, there are enough historical documents to attempt to recreate a model of a catapult that probably has similar construction and characteristics.

Ludgar, The War Wolf

👓 *Adult supervision required*

🪜 Swinging arm alert: Watch out for moving arms or levers

⚒ Sharp and/or heavy tool advisory: Project requires use of saw or hammer

⬤ Flying object alert: Use care when aiming and firing

The European catapults of the Middle Ages were often very large and played key roles in many sieges and battles. The trebuchet was the largest and most powerful of all the catapult types.

Unlike a ballista, this type of catapult fires its missiles in a high arcing trajectory, tracing out a parabola in the sky. Trebuchets could be built on a very large scale and were able to throw heavy, hard stones a long way, from well beyond the range of defensive archers and spear throwers.

This project is a model of a medieval trebuchet, similar to Ludgar, the War Wolf.

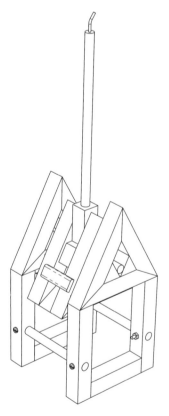

11.2 Ludgar, the War Wolf

MATERIALS

- Saw
- Hammer
- Nails or glue
- Drill
- ⅝-inch-diameter drill bit
- ³⁄₁₆-inch-diameter drill bit
- ½-inch-diamter drill bit
- Sandpaper
- String

Frame

- (4) 1-inch by 1-inch by 6-inch pieces of pine (Frame Uprights)
- (2) ½-inch-diameter, 6-inch-long wooden dowels (Frame Dowels)
- (2) 1-inch by 1-inch by 4-inch pieces of pine (Bottom Horizontal Crossbraces)
- (6) 1-inch by 1-inch by 6-inch pieces of pine, angle cut (Counterweight Support Members)
- (4) 1-inch by 1-inch by 1-inch pieces of wood, triangle cut (Pivot Holders)
- (4) #8 machine screws, 1½ inches long, and nuts
- (1) ⅝-inch-diameter, 6-inch-long dowel (Pivot Dowel)

Counterweight and Arm Assembly

- (1) ¹⁄₁₆-inch or ⅛-inch diameter bent wire (Release Hook)
- (1) ⅝-inch-diameter wooden dowel, 13 inches long (Throwing Arm)
- (1) 1-inch by 1-inch by 2½-inch piece of wood (Arm Holder)
- (7) 1-inch by 1-inch by 6-inch pieces of pine, with ends cut at 30 degrees (Counterweight Frame)
- (1) 1-inch by 1-inch by 3-inch piece of pine (Counterweight Cross Piece)
- (6) Moldings, ½-inch by ½-inch wood, various lengths

DIRECTIONS

General Notes

1. It is important to cut all of the wooden pieces to the sizes shown as accurately and as squarely as possible. Sand each one with sandpaper after cutting to smooth them and remove splinters.
2. The fit between holes and dowels will be tight, which is OK, but the counterweight must swing freely. If any hole is too tight, enlarge the hole with sandpaper or a file. You can also enlarge or "hog out" the hole by holding your drill at slight angles as you drill.
3. Wooden pieces may be attached to one another by using nails, glue, wooden dowels, or any combination thereof.
4. The assembly diagrams are critical to understanding how everything fits together. The exploded diagram at **diagram 11.3** shows how all the parts will eventually fit together.

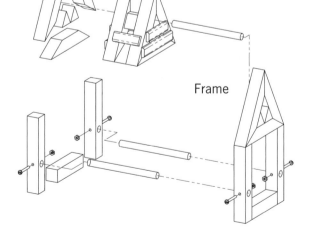

Throwing Arm

Counterweight

Frame

11.3

BUILDING THE FRAME

1. Cut all of the wooden pieces to the sizes shown in the materials list. Take great care when using the saw to cut the ends of the pieces off squarely and accurately. Note: some pieces require ends cut at angles of 30 and 60 degrees. Use a protractor to mark the angles with a pencil before you cut. Lightly sand the pieces if necessary.

2. Carefully drill four ½-inch diameter holes for the Frame Dowels in the Frame Uprights, 2 inches from the bottom ends. Remove wood splinters if necessary with sandpaper.

3. Insert a Frame Dowel into one of the holes you just drilled in a Frame Upright and push it until the end is flush with the far sides of the hole. Repeat the process with another Frame Upright and the other end of the same dowel.

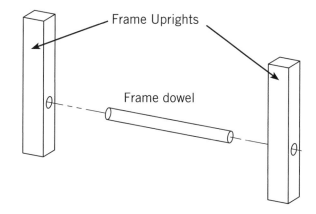

11.4

4. While both Frame Uprights are on a table, standing vertical and connected by the dowel, drill a ³⁄₁₆-inch hole through each Upright/Dowel intersection, as shown.

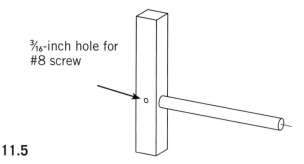

11.5

5. Connect the Uprights and frames using a #8 machine screw and nut, 1½-inches long, through the drilled hole.

6. Repeat Steps 3 through 5 with the remaining three Frame Uprights and Frame Dowel.

7. Build two complete "upper triangles" for the Frame, fastening the three pieces securely using small nails and glue. Each triangle is built from three equally long 4-inch wooden pieces made from 1-inch square wood. (Square and round wooden stock is often available at home stores and craft stores.) Cut a 30-degree angle at each end of each piece as shown. Attach the three pieces to form a close-fitting triangle using glue and nails.

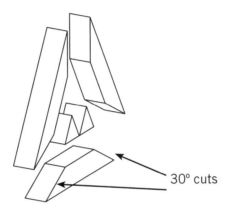

11.6

30° cuts

8. Glue the small triangular wooden shapes that form the support for the pivot to the bottom of each triangle as shown here.

9. Complete the side supports by attaching the rectangular Lower Support pieces and the Uprights and Dowels to the upper triangle with glue or nails (or both).

ASSEMBLING THE COUNTERWEIGHT

1. Drill a ⅝-inch-diameter hole in the center of the end of the Arm Holder to accommodate the Throwing Arm.

11.7

2. Drill a ⅝-inch-diameter hole in the center of the Counterweight Cross Piece. The Pivot Dowel is inserted in this hole and the whole Counterweight and Throwing Arm assembly rotates on it. The shape of the Counterweight's Cross Piece and the location of the hole are detailed in **diagram 11.8**.

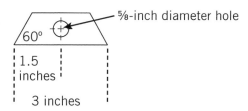

11.8

3. Nail and glue the pieces that make up two outer triangles of the Counterweight Frame together. One is shown in **diagram 11.9**. These two identical triangles will make up the exterior of the counterweight.

11.9

4. Place the final Frame Member between the triangles on the bottom and the Arm Holder on top.

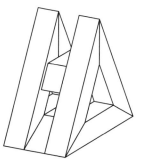

11.10

5. Insert the Counterweight Cross Piece where shown in **diagram 11.3** and nail and glue into place.

6. Insert a weight inside the triangle frames of the Counterweight. Rolls of coins, fishing weights, or small rocks work well. Experiment with different types of weights to see which works the best. Up to a point, the heavier the Counterweight, the better it generally works. The weight must be located below the pivot.

7. Attach the moldings to the sides and bottom of the Counterweight with small nails or glue. The molding slats must hold the weight within the Counterweight. You will need to cut the molding to fit your Counterweight.

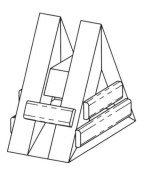

11.11

FINAL ASSEMBLY

1. Attach a nail to the top end of the Throwing Arm. The nail will connect the Sling to the Throwing Arm.

11.12

2. Insert the Throwing Arm into the hole in the Arm Holder and glue into place.

3. Now place the Counterweight Assembly inside the Frame Assembly and slide the Pivot Dowel into place.

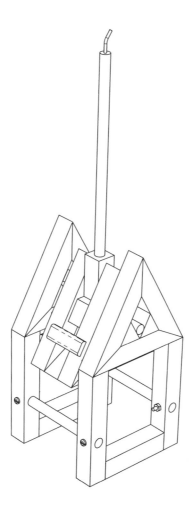

11.13

4. Make a Sacrificial Sling (one in which the sling is meant to be part of the projectile and is hurled along with the payload) by tying or gluing a length of string to the chosen projectile. Put a loop in the open end and slip it over the release hook. You will need to experiment with loop sizes and string lengths to figure out what works the best. Start with each piece of string approximately half the length of the throwing arm. When the throwing arm rotates, the loop should fly off the nail during rotation and fling the missile up and out in a big, round arc.

OPERATING THE TREBUCHET

1. Cock the trebuchet by pulling the Throwing Arm back.
2. Place an appropriately sized projectile consisting of payload and Sacrificial Sling on the release hook. A ½- to 1-inch round wooden ball works nicely.
3. Release the arm. If you've made the sling correctly, the trebuchet will shoot the missile in a high looping arc. Experiment with the sling to find the optimum length.

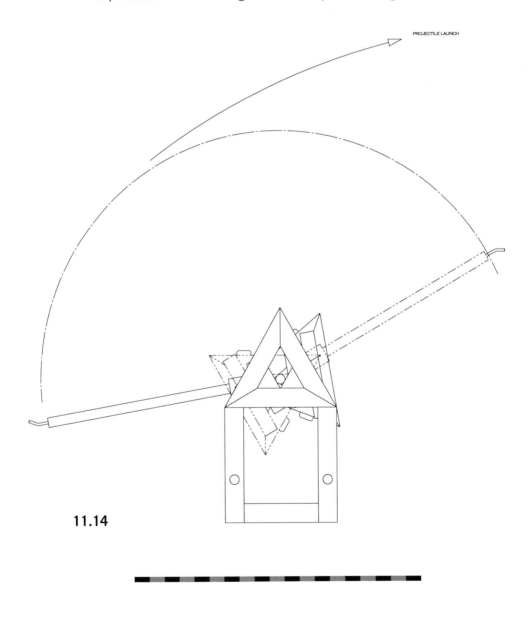

PROJECTILE LAUNCH

11.14

THE SUN SETS ON CATAPULT WARFARE

hy did armies stop using catapults? They stopped because cannons and gunpowder were invented; but it took a while for cannons to become popular. If someone were to have asked the King of Italy's top military officers if gunpowder artillery looked like a good idea when it first appeared at Florence in 1326, they might well have said, "Let's not bother with it." For at that time, armies all over Europe, the Middle East, and the Far East were having good luck making and using trebuchets and other types of catapults effectively.

If the officers compared those early cannons and bombards with the elegant trebuchets then in use, the comparison would not have made gunpowder weapons look attractive. At that time, cannons were crude, cumbersome, and inefficient. They were built from hard-to-find and hard-to-manufacture metal, so they were costly to make. Even more costly was the need to supply them with the rare, almost magical, alchemical propellant called Chinese Powder, which we now call gunpowder.

Also, those first cannons could not be aimed with nearly the accuracy of a well-made trebuchet; they could rarely hit the same spot on a castle wall twice, for the poor quality of the gunpowder made repeatable shooting impossible. Even worse, when gunpowder was transported, the inevitable shaking and vibration of the trip made the lighter charcoal particles rise to the top, with the result that early gunpowder had to be carefully remixed just before it was used: a perilous process and a time waster during battle conditions. You'd certainly think that any rational military commander in the early fourteenth century considering whether to use a trebuchet or a cannon would have found the decision to stick with the tried and true trebuchet an easy one.

But by the end of the century, a mere 75 years later, trebuchets were just about gone, almost completely replaced by rudimentary cannons, bombards, and musket-like arquebuses. Why was that? It's hard to say, but one thing is certain, gunpowder was a lot more fun. When a field commander fired a cannon, it made a terrific, resounding roar. The barrel flashed with fire and smoke. It was wonderful, impressive, and just the sort of justifiable extravagance that medieval kings and princes loved. Using a cannon in warfare became a symbol of modernity and progressiveness. A trebuchet may have been more efficient and maybe even more effective against castle walls, but in terms of vanity, visibility, and a good royal image, a gunpowder-based artillery brigade was, hands down, a more modern and desirable image for a prince than a trebuchet.

So, at about the time of the start of the Renaissance, around 1400 CE, all of the catapults discussed here—the elegant ballistae, the workhorse onagers, the simple traction catapults, and the gigantic trebuchets—were slowly replaced by the more modern technology of cannon and gunpowder. The switch did not happen overnight, and for a hundred years catapults were still in use, but as the years passed they became far less common.

Perhaps the last occasion on which a trebuchet was employed in a battle or siege was in 1480 at a siege on the island of Rhodes. The Greeks and their ancient enemy, the Turks, were fighting. The Turks attacked the Greek island town of Rhodes with their primitive cannons. Out of desperation, with their backs to the sea, the Rhodian defenders built a trebuchet. Historical accounts tell us that it was a fairly effective weapon, as it did more damage to the Turkish attackers than the Turkish cannons did to Rhodes.

There was one final instance of catapult warfare. It did not occur in the Levant, or Europe, or even in China. It happened in 1521 in Mexico, when the Spanish Conquistadors under Hernando Cortez marched on the Aztecs in what is now Mexico City. When the Spaniards ran low on ammunition for their cannons, one of Cortez's soldiers designed and built a trebuchet to continue the siege. According to the writings of Bernal Diaz, one of Cortez's lieutenants, it was a spectacular failure. The soldier, who claimed to have learned the art of catapult building in Italy as a young man, actually knew little about what it takes to design and build a trebuchet.

When Cortez's catapult was fired, it hurled its missile high into the air, but straight up. The great stone projectile landed right on top of the trebuchet itself and broke it. Cortez was livid and ordered what was left of the machine taken apart. There is no mention of what happened to the foolish soldier. And on this strange note, so ends the history of catapults in modern warfare.

Today, missile-firing catapults are still frequently built, but for show and fun instead of making war. Very large, elaborate catapults are used to entertain crowds at medieval theme fairs, to see who can toss a pumpkin the farthest in a contest, and just for the fun of making and using them.

The last catapult project is a simple project creating a game that is surprisingly fun to play.

Basket-Pult

Adult supervision required

Sharp and/or heavy tool advisory: Project requires use of saw or hammer

Flying object alert: Use care when aiming and firing

You can have a lot of fun making and playing with the following game of skill. It's a tabletop game that is combination of catapults and basketball: Basket-Pult! With adult help, the equipment for this game can be completed in an hour or two. It is easy to build and fun to play, especially in one-on-one or two-on-two matches.

This type of device would be considered a tension catapult, because the energy used to toss the walnut comes from the flexing the spoon, and this makes it a tension spring. When you bend the spoon down, you add energy to the spring. When you release it, the energy is transferred to the walnut and off it goes.

12.1

MATERIALS

- Glue
- Pen
- Drill
- Handsaw
- Vise
- Base
- (1) 11-inch by 5½-inch piece of wood, 1 inch thick (Base)
- (2) ½-inch by ½-inch by 5½-inch pieces of wood (Footers)

Backboard

- (1) 5½-inch by 4½-inch by ½-inch piece of wood (Backboard)
- (1) 2½-inch by ½-inch by 12-inch piece of wood (Backboard Support)
- (4) hex nuts, ¼-inch diameter
- (1) 1½-inch by 4-inch U-bolt, ¼-inch diameter
- (2) 1½-inch wood screws

Spoon Thrower

- (1) 1-inch wooden dowel, 4 inches long
- (2) 2½-inch round head machine screws, 10-24 thread
- (2) machine screw nuts, 10-24 thread, with washers
- Plastic spoon

DIRECTIONS

The Base

1. The diagram here shows how the whole game fits together, but feel free to experiment with the dimensions of the wooden pieces if you want.
2. Affix the two Footers to the Base using glue or wood screws. Each Footer should be 1½ inches from the long ends of the Base.

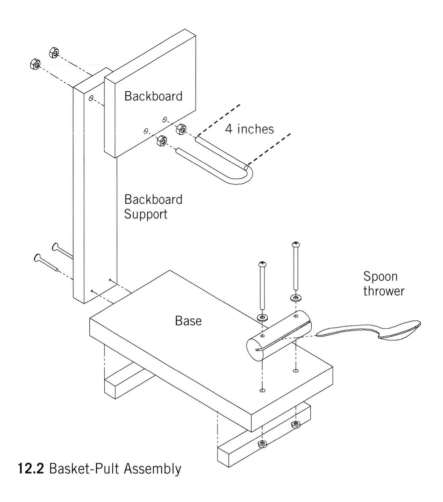

Backboard

4 inches

Backboard
Support

Spoon
thrower

Base

12.2 Basket-Pult Assembly

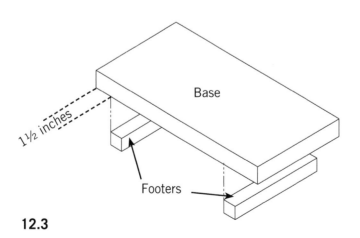

Base

1½ inches

Footers

12.3

The Backboard

1. Use the U-bolt and a pen to mark the location of two holes to
    be drilled ½ inch from the bottom of the Backboard, centered.
    Mark another two spots to drill holes at the top of the Backboard
    Support, ½ inch from the top.

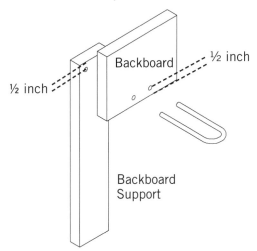

Backboard

½ inch

½ inch

Backboard
Support

12.4

2. Drill four ½-inch holes, two through the Backboard and two
    through the Backboard Support, at the marks.
3. Attach the U-bolt to the Backboard and Support using the four
    hex nuts as shown.

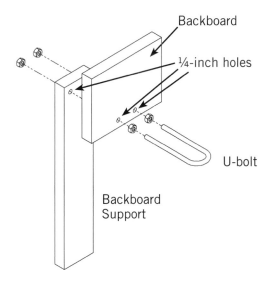

Backboard

¼-inch holes

U-bolt

Backboard
Support

12.5

4. Screw the entire Backboard assembly to the Base using two wood screws.

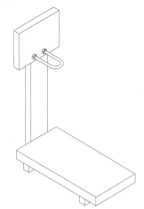

12.6

Spoon Thrower

1. Using a handsaw and a vise, carefully cut a ½-inch-deep groove into the wooden dowel, lengthwise. It should be just wide enough to insert the spoon's handle.

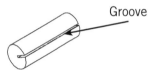

Groove

12.7

2. Reposition the dowel in a vise so that the groove angles up, 30 degrees from horizontal. Drill two vertical holes completely through the dowel, 1 inch from either end.

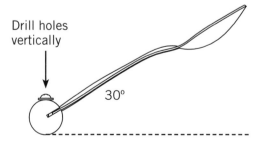

Drill holes vertically

30°

12.8

3. Use the dowel holes to mark two holes onto the base, 1 inch from the end opposite the Backboard.

4. Affix the dowel to the base using the machine screws and nuts, as shown.

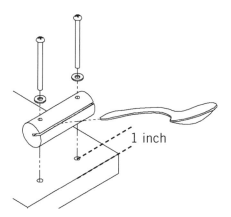

1 inch

12.9

5. Insert the spoon handle into the dowel groove. You're now ready to play!

RULES OF BASKET-PULT

The game is divided up into four quarters. Players earn points by hitting the rim with the projectile (worth one point) or shooting the projectile through or onto the hoop (worth three points).

Quarter 1: Each player shoots five whole walnuts. The game requires you use five different walnuts.

Quarter 2: Each player shoots five whole filberts.

Quarter 3: Each player shoots five whole pecans.

Quarter 4: Each player shoots five Brazil nuts. Because Brazil nuts are so oddly shaped, they are more difficult. Therefore, each rim hit earns two points and each nut landing and staying on the rim or going through the hoop earns five points.

The person with the most points at the end of the game wins.

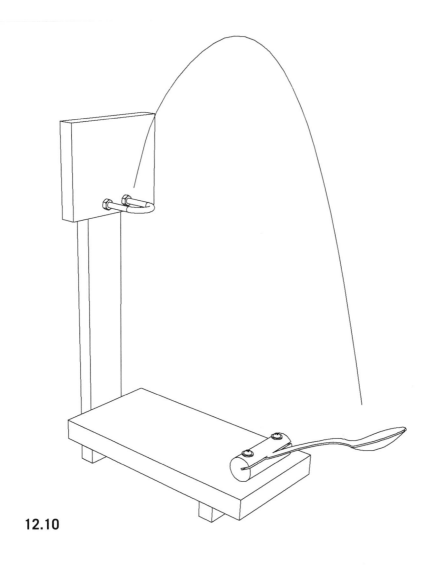

12.10

GLOSSARY

Artillery unit—a military group that sets up and operates cannons or catapults

Blockade—to encircle an enemy and prevent the delivery of supplies

Bolt—a short, heavy spear specifically made for a catapult or crossbow

Braccium—the moving arm of a catapult

Breach—an opening or hole in a wall

Buckler—a small round shield popular in medieval Europe

Cannon—a sturdy metal tube designed to shoot a projectile powered by an explosive propellant

Castellan—the man in charge or governor of a castle

Cavalry—a fighting group consisting of horse-mounted soldiers

Counterweight—a suspended weight attached to a pivoting catapult arm that causes it to swing

Garrison—a body of troops occupying a castle, fortress, or fortified town

Hegemony—the domination of one country over others

Howitzer—a medium-sized type of cannon

Incendiary—a chemical used to start fires

Infantry—the foot soldiers of an army

Levant—the geographical area of the eastern Mediterranean that is now occupied by Lebanon, Syria, and Israel

Master of Engines—the high-ranking soldier responsible for building and operating catapults

Mercenary—an unaligned soldier or fighting man whose services are secured by the payment of money

Missile—any object thrown from a catapult

Moat—a ditch, often filled with water, surrounding a castle as a means of defense

Quarter—to "give quarter" means to grant clemency to a captured enemy soldier and refrain from immediately putting him to death

Phalanx—an ancient formation of infantrymen in which closely packed and heavily armed soldiers brandish many long spears pointed straight ahead

Pike—a long spear with a small steel head, popular with medieval Scottish, Swiss, and Flemish fighters

Rampart—a walkway on the top of a castle wall from which defenders can fight

Rout—to defeat an opponent completely

Rules of engagement—the directives issued by the leaders of armies that state the circumstances under which their fighting forces will begin, continue, and end combat

Scutula—the wooden frame of a Roman catapult

Siege tower—a mobile wooden tower erected to allow soldiers to climb over castle walls during a siege

Tireme—a warship of ancient Greece, powered by oarsmen

Tonus—the rope torsion spring for a Roman catapult

ACKNOWLEDGMENTS

I gratefully acknowledge the help, advice, and contributions from Casimir Sienkiewicz, Grigg Mullen, Jane Dystel, Cynthia Sherry, Michelle Williams, the many readers of my previous books who took time to write me with suggestions and ideas, and of course, my friends and family.

BIBLIOGRAPHY

Allmand, Christopher. *Society at War—The Experience of England and France During the Hundred Years War*. Woodbridge, Suffolk, United Kingdom: The Boydell Press, 1998.
Explores in detail the impact of war on English and French society in the late Middle Ages.

Bradbury, Jim. *The Medieval Siege*. Woodbridge, Suffolk, United Kingdom: Boydell Press, 1992.
Describes the science and practice of medieval siegecraft, and the political importance of siege warfare.

Bradbury, Jim. *Philip Augustus King of France 1180–1223*. New York: Longman Press, 1998.
Biography of the 12th-century French king that describes his conflicts with the English crown, including Richard I and John.

De Camp, L. Sprague. *The Ancient Engineers*. Garden City, NY: Doubleday, 1963.
An accessible history of the great engineering feats of the human race up to the Renaissance.

Payne Gallwey, Sir Ralph. *The Crossbow, Medieval and Modern, Military and Sporting: Its Construction, History and Management*. London: Longmans, Green, and Co., 1903.
Surveys the history and management of the crossbow, and documents the development of ancient and medieval siege engines.

Verbruggen, J. F. *Art of Warfare in Western Europe During the Middle Ages*. Amsterdam, Netherlands: North Holland Publishing Co., 1977.
A scholarly description of warfare of the Middle Ages, written by a Belgian historian with descriptions of famous battles.

Warner, Philip. *Sieges of the Middle Ages*. New York: Barnes and Noble Books, 1994.
Describes English sieges from the Norman Conquest to the end of the War of the Roses.

Warry, John. *Warfare in the Classical World.* New York: Barnes and
Nobles Books, 1993.
*Traces the evolution of the art of war in the Greek and Roman
worlds between 1600 BCE and 800 CE.*

INDEX